FACE TO FACE
POLAR PORTRAITS

FACE TO FACE
POLAR PORTRAITS

HUW LEWIS-JONES

SCOTT POLAR RESEARCH INSTITUTE
University of Cambridge

Published in association with
POLARWORLD

First published in Great Britain in 2008

Published by Polarworld on behalf of the Scott Polar Research Institute

Scott Polar Research Institute
University of Cambridge
Lensfield Road
Cambridge CB2 1ER

Designed by Liz House
Printed and bound in Italy by Graphicom, FSC certified company

FRONT COVER: Cecil Meares, by Herbert Ponting, 1912

FRONT MONTAGE, pp. 6-7
Top left to bottom right: British adventurer Pen Hadow displays his polar kit, 2003; *Terra Nova* framed in the distance from within a cavern in a stranded iceberg, 5 January 1911. Ponting was captivated by this grotto, writing that it was 'the most wonderful place imaginable'; Ben Saunders, equipment testing in Resolute Bay, 2008; Herbert Ponting, 30 January 1912; 'Emperor and Mule', a photograph by Frank Debenham, 1911; Ann Daniels, Halloween, Ellesmere Island, 2008; Pan hopping in Lake Fjord, second British Arctic Air Route expedition, 1932-33; Small man, large iceberg, Qikiqtarjuaq, 2004; Rosie Stancer, Resolute Bay, 2007; Quentin Riley, meteorologist on the British Arctic Air Route expedition, 1930-31; The Patriot Hills radio tent, Antarctica, 2003; Survey aeroplane being towed into open water, British Arctic Air Route expedition, 1930-31; Krisravista and the gramophone, Captain Scott's *Terra Nova* expedition, 1910-13; Martin Hartley on ice, 86 degrees, Canadian Arctic Ocean, 2006; Dr Alexander Macklin with the dogs, Shackleton's *Endurance* expedition, 1915; Pen Hadow, Antarctica, 2003

REAR MONTAGE, pp. 286-87
Top left to bottom right: Sir Ranulph Fiennes, Italian Alps, 2005; Henry Rennick and 'a friendly Adelie', 9 February 1911; Mi-6 helicopter at the Military base on Sredniy Island, 2004; Herbert Ponting and his telephoto apparatus, January 1912; 'Captain Scott in his den', Cape Evans, 7 October 1911; View from a hotel near the River Khatanga, March 2004; 'Watering ship', carrying snow on board, *Discovery* expedition, 1901-04; Nick Cutcliffe standing on blue iceberg off the coast of Qikiqtarjuaq, 2002; Mary Qulitalik, star of the film *Atanarjuat*, waits in Igloolik Airport, 17 March 2008; 'Some of the Landing Party', *Discovery* expedition, 1901-04; Ben Saunders pulling his sledge at sunset, 2004; The surgeon Dr Edward Atkinson in his small laboratory, *Terra Nova* expedition, 15 September 1911. 'Atkinson is quietly pursuing the subject of parasites ... already he is in a new world'; Some of Scott's men 'enjoying lunch in the tent', 7 January 1911; Lady walking across main square in Khatanga, Northern Siberia, March 2004; Sledge party on skis, *Nimrod* expedition, 1907-09; Modern polar travellers, Patric Woodhead, Alastair Vere Nicholl and Paul Landry, Antarctica, 2004

ISBN: 978-0-901021-08-3 (soft-cover)
ISBN: 978-0-901021-07-6 (hardback)

The book accompanies a touring exhibition that opened in Cambridge, England during the summer of 2008, and which will be displayed in select galleries in the United Kingdom and North America

The Publisher would like to thank Arctic Kingdom and Arctic Paper for their support of this book

PREVIOUS PAGE: The photographer Herbert Ponting posing for a polar portrait in Antarctica, January 1912. He provided his own caption, scribbled in pencil: 'Ponting cooling his head'.

RIGHT: A.E. Staley camera, used by Captain Robert Scott at the South Pole in 1912.

www.spri.cam.ac.uk   www.polarworld.co.uk   www.arctickingdom.com   www.arcticpaper.com   www.fsc.org

CONTENTS

LEFT: Modern adventurer
Pen Hadow training
for his North Pole Solo
expedition, Resolute
Bay, 2003.

FOLLOWING PAGE:
Having unloaded
supplies, Captain Scott,
Edward Wilson and
Teddy Evans make the
long trek back across the
pack ice to *Terra Nova*,
9 January 1911.

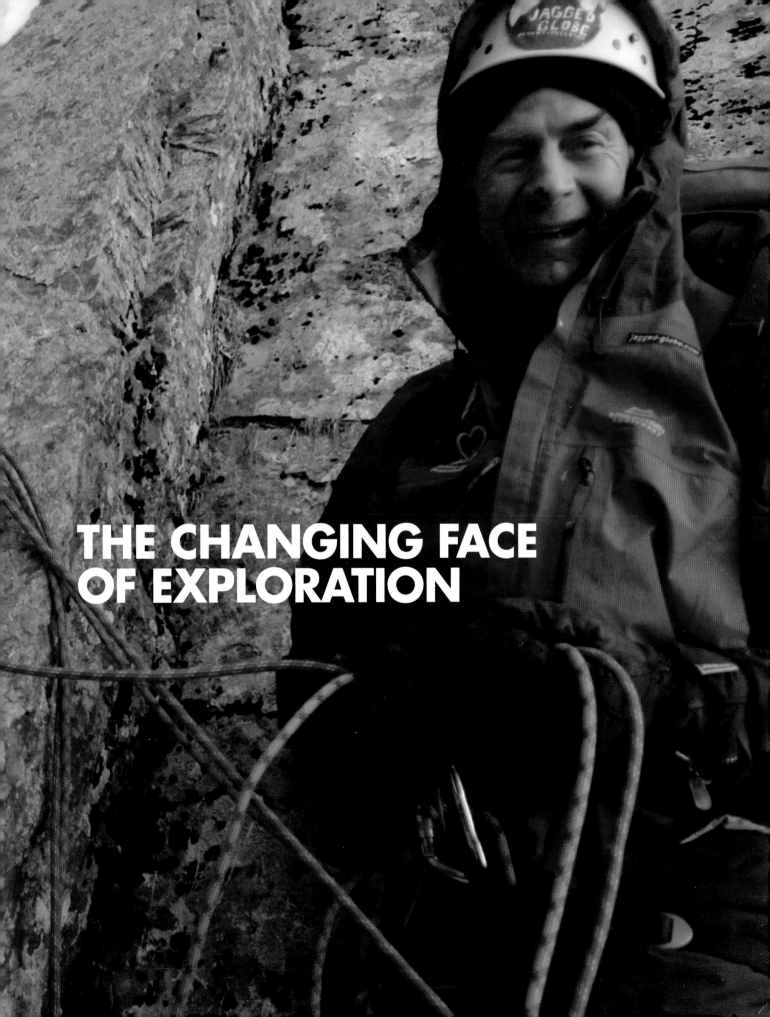

THE CHANGING FACE
OF EXPLORATION

PREVIOUS PAGE:
Sir Ranulph Fiennes
shares a joke with his
climbing companions,
Italian Alps, 2005.

ABOVE: Captain Scott
and his party at the
South Pole, 1912. He
later wrote: 'All the day
dreams must go ...
Great God! This is an
awful place'.

BELOW: Henry 'Birdie'
Bowers' first attempt
at this polar portrait,
published here for the
first time.

In a world, which is expanding day by day, literature is no longer enough ... our busy age does not always have time to read, but it always has time to look.

THÉOPHILE GAUTIER, 1858

FOREWORD

THE CHANGING FACE OF EXPLORATION

SIR RANULPH FIENNES

The South Pole was an awful place to be on 18 January 1912. Captain Scott and his four companions – Wilson, Bowers, Oates, and Evans – had just found that the Norwegian explorer Amundsen had beaten them to the prize one month earlier. The photograph that the men took that day speaks volumes for their achievement, of course, but there could be no truer record of their total disappointment. The men look absolutely broken; a photograph on top of everything else seems like a punishment. They are utterly devastated. A life's ambition has been snatched from their grasp. Now 800 miles from their base, they dragged themselves northward into the mouth of a raging blizzard. Their photographs and letters home, recovered with their bodies some time later, tell the sad tale of their sacrifice.

On 15 December 1980 I also stood for the first time at the South Pole and forced a smile for the cameras. This was the opening chapter of our Transglobe Expedition. It was a moment of huge relief, of course, but the real challenge was yet to come. We were aiming at the first polar circumnavigation of the Earth. We turned our faces to the north and hauled our sledges onward. It was not until April 1982 that we finally reached the North Pole. By that time a photograph was the last thing on our mind. I have experienced the polar world in all of its ferocity, when it is a challenge just to stay alive, let alone pull out a camera and take a photograph.

The Scott Polar Research Institute (SPRI) was founded in 1920 as a memorial to those men who died returning from the South Pole. It is the oldest international centre for polar research. Among so many recent successes, it was fitting that in 2004, with the help of the Heritage Lottery Fund,

SPRI was able to acquire over 1,700 of Herbert Ponting's original large-format glass plate negatives. They even have the old Staley camera that captured the despair of Scott's arrival at the South Pole, and some of Ponting's Antarctic gear. I didn't have to think twice when I considered where would be the best home for the photographs of my past polar expeditions.

I have just donated the entire archive of my Transglobe Expedition to SPRI and yet more objects will follow, including the camera equipment from many of my travels. The FREEZE

Though the face of exploration has changed so much in recent years, the pull of the polar regions is inescapable.

FRAME programme at SPRI is digitising over 20,000 historic images from its photographic collections: a vast visual treasure of many decades of expeditioning and scientific work in the polar regions. They also have ambitious plans to redevelop their galleries. The new Polar Museum is due to open in 2010. This is a busy and exciting time for SPRI.

Ponting is one of those men that you simply must admire. His photographs of Scott's *Terra Nova* expedition of 1910-13 are among the finest ever obtained in the Antarctic. Even today few are able to match the mastery with which he aimed his lens. Cherry-Garrard, author of *The Worst Journey in the World*, wrote: 'He came to do a job, did it and did it well. Here in these pictures is beauty linked to tragedy – and the beauty is inconceivable for it is endless and runs to eternity'. Ponting devoted the rest of his life to publicising the achievements of Scott's fateful expedition, to make sure that they had not died in vain. His photographs are a stunning visual legacy to this Heroic Age of Antarctic exploration; moments so far removed from our comfortable world of satellite navigation, high tech equipment, and almost certain rescue.

I must congratulate Dr Huw Lewis-Jones, who conceived this project, on gathering together such a fine collection of modern and historic photography. This book, and the travelling exhibition that accompanies it, does huge credit to the legacy of the achievements of these pioneers of the past. Among so many projects he seems to juggle, he is a historian and the new Curator of Art at SPRI, and a lucky fellow to boot, being able to work with such unique and world-class polar collections.

Not merely recovering some of the treasured Ponting and Hurley photographs, Huw has dug deep into the archives and now brings forward some absolutely stunning images. We see here some of the very first polar photographs and rare images of many figures

long forgotten by recent history books. We see men and women of many different nations, exploring, living, doing science, perhaps even holidaying amongst the ice. Almost all of the imagery here – some from personal albums, private collections, and a fleet of new commissions – has never been before the public eye.

One of my favourites, which I borrow for this Foreword, shows Scott as a young naval officer in 1901, shortly before leaving for his first polar expedition. Little could he know how the years ahead would play out. You can almost breathe his optimism that morning onboard *Discovery*. Behind him is a youthful-looking merchant officer by the name of Ernest Shackleton and beside him stands an aged man with splendid white whiskers. That is Admiral Sir Francis Leopold McClintock, a veteran of the old nineteenth-century Arctic voyages: a polar hero long before these young gents were even born. Photographs have the ability to transport us back in time effortlessly, and they do get so much better with age. I am delighted to be able to support this wonderful project.

Martin Hartley has chased me with his camera all over the world. He recently joined me in climbing a frozen waterfall: the day, in fact, when he secured my portrait for this book. I was training for an assault of Everest. He won't admit it, but Martin was struggling to keep up. He was much pleased with the dribble of blood across my face, the result of a large piece of falling ice. Little does the viewer know, until now I suppose, that Martin was also absolutely plastered in his own blood, injured as he hacked away at the ice as he scrambled up behind me. Ah, the perils of portraiture.

Having been on 17 assignments in the polar regions, Martin more than most knows what it takes to be out in the wilderness. His photographs are certainly among the best from today's technological world. Modern expeditions are now wrapped around with media coverage so the value of having good photographs is obvious. Just like those pioneering cameramen who went before him, his images are embracing and they lead us into the beautiful spaces of the polar regions. Whether showing joy, courage, doubt, or sheer desperation, portraits can tell us so much about the hopes and the failures that attend polar exploration. Though the face of exploration has changed so much in recent years, the pull of the polar regions is inescapable. You may meet many explorers for the first time in the pages of this book. Enjoy the experience, but don't dwell in your armchair too long. Be inspired, get outdoors. Alone in the wilderness, you'll come face to face with things that are impossible to imagine.

Exmoor, 2008

RIGHT: Scott appears on the deck of *Discovery*, his first polar command, on 5 August 1901. The ship was at Cowes, shortly before leaving England, to receive a visit by King Edward VII, Queen Alexandra and Princess Victoria. Sir Clements Markham and Admiral Sir Francis Leopold McClintock were also in the party shown around the ship that morning. Scott is proudly wearing the Royal Victorian Order, which the King had presented to him moments before this photograph was taken.

PHOTOGRAPHY THEN

The outfit for an explorer should be:-
Camera with one or two lenses.
Extra lenses should be taken for safety on long expeditions.
At least 4 dark slides. (See that they all work easily on the camera, and keep them as much sheltered from the sun as possible to prevent their warping. It is desirable to keep them wrapped up in black or yellow cloth or oil-silk.)
1 small store-box, as above.
Larger store-boxes, as many as may be required.
Stand, according to circumstances.
2 or 3 clamps to fix camera to stand.
Plate for taking stereoscopic views, if the camera will admit of such being taken.
Some black velvet or cloth, and plenty of india-rubber bands for holding the velvet over the camera.

HINTS TO TRAVELLERS, **1878**

ESSAY
PHOTOGRAPHY THEN
HUW LEWIS-JONES

Sir John Franklin is the first. The sun is high. He adjusts his cocked hat, bound with black silk, and gathers up his telescope. The buttons on his Captain's uniform seem desperate to break free from the strain of his ample belly. He shifts uncomfortably in his chair, positioned on the deck of the stout ship *Erebus*, as she wallows at her moorings in the London docks. It is 1845. The photographer, Richard Beard, urges the explorer to stay still for just a moment longer. He removes the lens cap, he waits, another minute, and then swiftly slots it back in place. The first polar photographic portrait is secured.

Other senior officers of the exploration ships *Erebus* and *Terror* had their photographs taken that day, optimistically submitting themselves to the photographer's eye. They appear to us now as if frozen in time. So, too, they followed Sir John Franklin as he led them in search of a navigable northwest passage, into the maze of islands and straits which forms the

Canadian Arctic. At Franklin's request, Beard supplied the expedition with a complete photographic apparatus, which was safely stowed aboard the well-stocked ship, alongside other technological marvels: portable barrel-organs, tinned meat and soups, an inflatable rubber boat, scientific equipment, the twenty-horse-power engines loaned from the Greenwich railway and a library of over twelve hundred volumes. The camera now formed part of the kit thought essential to travel to the limits of the known world. Weighed down with stores, yet buoyant with Victorian confidence, the expedition sailed from the Thames on 19 May. The ships were last seen in late July, making their way northward in Baffin Bay, before vanishing without a trace.

With these early photographs we start our journey. In a small gesture, they mark the beginning of a passage from high art to the production of a visual culture on a grand scale, a departure point in an expanding realm of representation that brought the

PREVIOUS PAGE: The 'Western geological party', *Terra Nova* expedition, 1910-13. From left to right are Robert Forde, Frank Debenham, Griffith Taylor and Tryggve Gran. Debenham was the founding Director of the Scott Polar Research Institute in 1920.

LEFT: Sir John Franklin daguerreotype, the first polar portrait, 1845.

wonders of the world and those who travelled to its outer reaches, before the public eye as never before. This moment might be hard to imagine in our image-saturated lives, where the imprint of the photograph is everywhere, in a world where our modern cameras are mini computers, where telephones are themselves cameras. Yet, on this sunny morning in 1845, we meet a new technology soon to take over the globe. Just over a hundred years later, the first photographs were taken in space, and soon after this a new generation of explorers would send back images from the surface of the moon.

Photographs, clearly, have a life of their own and can go on remarkable journeys. Over a long career a single image can have a great many meanings. They travel, they are used, perhaps manipulated, presented in new ways, and endlessly reinterpreted. Rather than simply

> Does an explorer need to appear frostbitten and adventurous to be seen as heroic, and do we require faces like these to imagine their achievement?

looking, it is of course possible to *read* a photograph, not only as an image but also as a *text*. That reading (in fact, any reading) involves a series of difficult, and often ambiguous, relationships between the reader and the image. Even images as seemingly simple as a portrait are layered with many possible forms of understanding. This book of images – a collection of pictures, a big polar facebook – urges this sort of multiple reading. A photograph has been selected, above all, for its merit as a great photograph, but what exactly makes a photograph *great*, anyway?

This choice of photographs is a response to my understanding of what I want to see in a polar portrait; how, perhaps, I imagine explorers and those people who live and work in the polar world. But this *selection* is, by its very definition, a limited view, incomplete, inconsistent, partial. How does one choose 50 portraits, from a rich historical collection that could yield many, many more: where even to begin? In response, how then to pick 50 modern portraits, from a modern portfolio whilst also identifying gaps, individuals perhaps forgotten, but whose lives and achievements demand our attention. The expedition photographer Martin Hartley rose to this challenge and we commissioned many new portraits to complete this selection. But, we both realise, this is simply the

beginning, the first step in a visual chronicle, through portraiture, of the men and women who have spent long careers amongst the ice.

How exactly do we direct our gaze? Does an explorer need to appear frostbitten and adventurous to be seen as heroic and do we require faces like these to imagine their achievement? Photographs are naturally nostalgic, but does it become obvious when idealism gets in the way of a truthful picture? Romance and frankness do not often sit well together. Where does accuracy end and parody begin and, indeed, does this really matter? The act of being photographed produces an unnatural state of things, no matter how much we might imagine it to be a mirror of something that actually happened. The art of the photograph is artefact. We might ask why would an individual want to pose in this way, in presenting themselves to the world? We may like to know why and perhaps exactly *how* has the photographer obtained such a response? Coming face to face with explorers in this way, through the photographer's vision and the camera's lens, what are we really seeing, and does it change the way we think about both the memory and the reality of exploration?

Clearly, photographs are materials of history – they remind us of stories, they represent facts, they memorialise as much as they enliven. They are fragments of history, brief glimpses of the past. However, face to face with these old photographs, the modern image takes on new meaning. We are able to judge, we can reappraise, we can, quite simply, enjoy ourselves. To qualify as a *polar* portrait, we might ask whether an image needs to be taken whilst an explorer is battling against the elements, or perched precariously on an ice floe? Some of these photographs, as in the case of Franklin's, were captured before an expedition's departure – a great many more were taken after the return home, at the height of fame, perhaps ignominy, after success or even miserable failure. A few even present explorers in their homes; the heroes of the great outdoors, indoors. We hope to begin to answer a few of these questions with this gallery of portraits, but we must not try too hard. This book is, after all, about one thing above everything else – it is a book created to display some stunning portraits. It may be best to leave the rest to the imagination.

Back in 1845, two sets of these pioneering photographs were made. Just before the ships left, one was presented as a keepsake to Franklin's wife, Lady Jane, whilst Beard kept the other set for reproduction in the newspapers, realising that polar portraits might turn a handsome

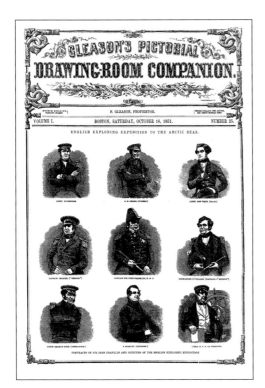

profit. As the search for the missing expedition – some 129 men in all – reached its height, these images found their way into homes and into the hearts of the public on both sides of the Atlantic who followed progress anxiously in the press, in illustrated lectures and in the books they bought. The polar portrait was, evidentially, a lucrative and emotive commodity. In the following years, over thirty expeditions were sent out in search of the lost party. 'The constant and never-failing efforts of Lady Franklin in her endeavours to send succour to her distant husband', ran the commentary in *Gleason's Companion*, 'has clothed the whole subject in a romantic garb'. McClintock's search expedition aboard the steam yacht *Fox*, financed largely by Lady Jane, found relics and written records and finally confirmed the fate of the Franklin party. However, the chapter was far from closed and the power of the story, and of the photograph, endures. Frozen in time, Franklin's portrait encourages us to open our eyes and to continue the search.

A FASHIONABLE NEW ART

Pausing for a moment to have his shoes cleaned at the side of a Parisian avenue, an unidentified man becomes the first ever to have his photograph taken. It is late in

1838, or possibly early the following year. High above on the rooftops, Louis-Jacques-Mandé Daguerre has been aiming his camera for almost ten minutes. Hurrying pedestrians and the busy carriages on the Boulevard du Temple do not stop long enough to register on the image; they are merely indistinct smudges; the street looks deserted. To our modern eyes, the photo appears grainy, blurred, distorted, like the fellow's shoes perhaps, a little scuffed up. For photography, there would soon be shine and polish. As technologies improved, pioneering photographers became celebrated figures and very wealthy men. Within an increasingly visual culture the photograph was everywhere – fashionable, intriguing, sensational. It became a national pastime. As a medium it passed into art; it may be fairly said, that within a hundred years, 'photography had taken over the world'.

Photography's first big year was 1839. Simultaneous announcements of two processes for fixing an image directly from nature, using optical and chemical means, caused a wave of excitement in England and France and the news soon spread throughout the Western world. After many years of experimentation, Daguerre, a Parisian stage designer, declared the perfection of a process that produced an image on a silver-coated copper plate. Across the Channel, an English gentleman, William Henry Fox Talbot, revealed a positive-negative technique on paper that was destined to become the basis of modern photography. Both were united by a profound conceptual advance, ideally suited to the changing time – the face of nature could be imagined accurately, measured, possessed; enjoyed by all, captured for posterity. Photography presented a mirror to the world and was rightly heralded as the 'foundation of a new order of possibilities'.

After an autumn spent in Paris – being instructed by Daguerre himself – Antoine Claudet submitted the first specimens of this new art to be seen in Britain to Queen Victoria and Prince Albert and also showed the remainder of his portraits and continental streetscapes at soirées of the Royal Society in 1840. The daguerreotype portrait was such a fashionable curiosity during this year that people were willing to buy the images of total strangers – probably artists' models used to posing without moving, therefore able to endure the necessary ten minutes exposure. This was a new way of recording, but also a new way of *seeing* altogether. Initially the reserve of wealthy amateurs and inventors, photography soon became a lucrative profession as popular demand for images grew.

ABOVE: The lost explorers, Sir John Franklin and his officers, the first polar portraits to make front page news, *Gleason's Pictorial Drawing-Room Companion*, 18 October 1851.

Richard Beard, the pioneering photographer who captured Franklin's portrait before the explorer departed for an icy grave, was actually the first British licensee of Daguerre's process. Just as his competitor Claudet was experimenting on his sunny rooftop, Beard's portrait studio opened in 1841 at the Royal Polytechnic Institution in London. It was probably the first in Europe, and he entertained the great and the good for many years, all keen to participate in the new sensational art form. To Beard, who was originally a coal merchant, photography was a speculation, a means of getting rich quickly. He mastered the elaborate techniques required and by the end of the year it was reported that his new portraits were 'perfectly correct whatever may be the size in which they are taken, and the eyes appear beautifully marked and expressive'. When the springtime sunshine had chance to break through the London smog, exposure times had reduced to two or three minutes, a considerable advance. Novelty fuelled excitement and the masses soon flocked to Beard's establishment:

Like the crowds who repair / To Old Cavendish Square,
And mount up a mile and a quarter of stair
In procession that beggars the Lord Mayor's show!
And all are on tiptoe, the high and the low,
To sit in that glass-cover'd blue studio;
In front of those boxes, wherein when you look,

Your image reversed will minutely appear,
So delicate, forcible, brilliant and clear,
So small, full, and round, with a life so profound,
As none ever wore / In a mirror before ...

Excited though the crowds were, Beard was more so. Business was better than he could have imagined; the average takings each day are said to have amounted to something like £150. At the time the average skilled man earned no more than ten shillings (50p) a week, so such sums would have been beyond Beard's wildest dreams. However, it was not to last. With such rewards on offer, it was not long before competitors filled London's avenues with their own studios. Photographers were soon to be found on almost every street, a development that led some to question their contribution to the art: 'the appetites as well as the vanity of the public are stimulated by the offer of "an eel-pie and your likeness for a sixpence"'. Whichever way they were served, it was clear that photographic portraits meant big business, and both photographers and sitters drove up demand. It was Beard, and others like him, who created the public habit of being photographed. Within two years there were studios in almost every major town in Britain.

It was not merely the daguerreotype that heralded this new visual culture, but a vast array of technologies and an expanding audience hungry for spectacular

ART-PROGRESS.

Artist (!) "Now, Mum! Take orf yer 'ead for Sixpence, or yer 'ole body for a Shillin'!"

RIGHT: Photography, the fashionable sensation, hits the London streets, cartoon from *Punch*, 1857.

Hint for a Photographer's Tent.

Our Photographer invents a Tent.

images of the world and its peoples. Theatrical performances, grand circular panoramic paintings, canvases moving by pulleys and rolling wheels, optical illusions, magic lantern projections, and lectures illuminated by the flash of limelight all attracted wide audiences. Steam-driven printing presses powered this cycle of popular entertainment. In this new world image was everything and photography quickly joined the lively visual mix.

Fox Talbot's book, *The Pencil of Nature*, appeared in six parts beginning in June 1844, and may be fairly described as 'one of the most momentous photographic publications ever'. Its significance lies not so much in the fact that it was the first to contain photographic images, nor even that it was produced in huge numbers, but that it set up a visual point of reference amidst a bewildering new era, a guide for the way photography was to be viewed for much of the nineteenth century. Jabez Hogg's *Practical Manual of Photography* sold out immediately after it was published in 1843, and was soon reprinted. Maxime du Camp's stunning photographs of Egyptian temples and tombs along the Nile were published in Paris in 1852, marking another revolution in illustrated book publishing. The travelling-photographer had arrived and the geographical imagination never looked back.

In autumn 1847, London had its first Photographic Club, a union of keen amateurs and wealthy supporters who met a few times each month to compare results over supper and a glass of claret. Most were now practising Talbot's calotype process, a technique consisting of a piece of fine paper sensitized to light and exposed in the camera for about a minute. This paper negative was then developed immediately and the image fixed before being printed. Others continued to experiment with glass and eventually found that a thin layer of egg white (albumen) acted as a good coating to ensure that the silver salts would not dissolve or float off during development and fixing. This invention was a step forward but its slowness (five to fifteen minutes exposure, depending on the light) prevented its immediate use for portraiture, but it was excellent for landscapes and for recording the architecture of the nation's rapidly expanding towns.

The length of exposure could be considerably reduced if the plate was exposed immediately after sensitizing, while still moist, but this meant – at least for the travelling photographer – the inconvenience of carrying a dark-tent and chemicals. Joseph Nicéphore Niépce's view through an attic window of the courtyard of his country house, captured in 1826, probably lays claim to being the first photograph. It had taken almost eight hours of sunshine to expose on a polished pewter plate, so long in fact that there are shadows from both sides of the image as the sun passed overhead. For photography to become practical, exposure times simply had to improve.

Albumen was found also to be good for coating positive paper, and once gold chlorine toner had been devised (in 1852), portraits could appear in rich detail. Soon albumenized positive paper could be bought ready prepared, and the portrait business boomed into mass market. Such was the demand for albumen in the 1850s that factory farming of hens was introduced. At a time when demand for the cheap *carte-de-visite*

ABOVE: Photography, cumbersome yet the must-have travel accessory, cartoon from *Punch*, 1856.

ABOVE: *Carte-de-visite* of Sir James Clark Ross, veteran polar explorer, 1860.

Carte-de-visite of Sir Edward Sabine, polar scientist and President of the Royal Society, 1869.

pictures was at its peak, over half a million eggs were used annually by one London firm alone. Thirty years later, after Kodak had revolutionised amateur snap-shooting, the US photographic market was devouring 300 million eggs a year. To give yet more figures, it was estimated that between 3 and 4 million *cartes* were sold annually in England alone at the height of this 'cartomania' craze. These small silver prints, pasted onto card, were ideal for photographers to mass-produce, and inexpensive for consumers to collect. Individual portraits sold in staggering numbers. For instance, Downey's 1867 photograph of the Princess of Wales carrying her baby Princess Louise upon her back sold 300,000 copies, making it the most popular photograph then published in Britain.

The year of Daguerre's death, 1851, witnessed the beginning of a new period in photography. The great invention, which supplanted all existing methods, was Frederick Scott Archer's 'wet collodion' process, introduced in March of that year, so-called because the photographer had to do everything – coat the plate, expose it and then develop it – while it was wet. It was the fastest photographic process yet devised and won immediate popularity. However, it was still a tricky proposition. Taking a wet-plate photo still meant carrying a portable darkroom and a case of noxious chemicals, making remote location photography a difficult task. The still faster gelatin dry plate would only eclipse it some thirty years later. Up to about 1880, collodion was the most widely used technique. Even today, where digital has not won out totally, processors continue to use wet collodion.

The relaxation of Talbot's patent in July 1852 and the gradual perfection of the collodion process at last made photography a popular pursuit. The London School of Photography was founded in 1854 to cater to this new demand, providing teaching and instruction, whilst also making money to support itself by taking portraits. Lady Eastlake, wife of the first president of the new Photographic Society, summed up the growing photographic brotherhood:

Tens of thousands are now following a new business, practising a new pleasure, speaking a new language, and bound together by a new sympathy. For it is one of the pleasant characteristics of this pursuit that it unites men of the most diverse lives, habits, and stations, so that whoever enters its ranks finds himself in a kind of republic, where he needs apparently but to be a photographer to be a brother ...

By 1861 over two-dozen photographic societies had been established, with enthusiasts all over the country aiming their lenses at a changing Britain. Portrait photography had become an industry and the uses of photography were seen almost everywhere. In archaeology, as in construction, in the new sciences of meteorology and microscopy, photography became the essential tool of recording. Even Queen Victoria had a darkroom constructed at Windsor Castle and is said to have become very skilled in the 'black art' under the guidance of Dr Becker, Prince Albert's librarian. In 1860, her miniature portrait secured the *carte-de-visite's* fashionable status and started a frenzy of production. The Queen herself was to become an avid collector of photographs and, in time, large prints and engravings of her many photographic portraits came to be displayed in homes, school halls and railway stations throughout the Empire.

Even at this early stage, photographs could be retouched, altered, even 'beautified' with artistic effects. Two versions of the same portrait – one retouched, the other not – astounded crowds at the Exposition Universelle held in Paris in 1855. It was one of the world's first photographic exhibitions, and the news that the camera could lie made getting photographed much more popular. A typical advert for one 'photographist' claimed that he could change the shape of a nose, brush away wrinkles, or sculpt cheekbones so elegantly they would put the 'Venus de Medici' to shame. Another claimed that it was possible with expert tinting to give a gentleman an 'intellectual head', whilst another promised to perform wonders with a woman's figure, 'to slice off, or curve the lady's waist after his own idea of shape and form and size'.

Both curiosity and vanity drove this demand and, for those able to capitalise on the fashion, vast fortunes could be made. There was huge profit in photography overseas too, and it was soon pressed into foreign service. From 1856, photography was taught to young officers of the Royal Engineers at Chatham and later at other military and naval establishments. This training also proved invaluable for men serving in the East India Company, and for doctors and missionaries leaving Britain for the outposts of an expanding Empire.

Photography still ruled in the comfort of one's home. Collectable and fashionable, the walls and mantelpieces of Victorian parlours began to be populated by the photographic art. Affectionately collected, and proudly pasted to each page, family albums swelled with the faces of loved ones. No longer was photography an art for the privileged: it had become an art for the masses. 'Blessed be the inventor of photography', wrote Mrs Carlyle in 1859. 'I set him above even the inventor of chloroform! It has given more positive pleasure to poor suffering humanity than anything that has cast up in my time, or is like to – this art, by which even the poorest can possess themselves of tolerable likenesses of their absent dear ones'.

The photographic portrait, as now, helped to bring families together even when they were apart. It changed the way people looked at themselves and the world around them. This was a liberating invention, giving everyone a chance to escape the everyday, to travel the world, to dream of the exotic. In 1858, for example, the *Stereoscopic Magazine* was founded and each issue offered eager subscribers three new double images: photographs of ruined churches, new railway lines, classical sculptures, the grassy tumble of the Lakeland fells, perhaps a few sights of the European Grand tour, a spot of leopard hunting, maybe a leisurely afternoon in the company of some 'hindoo dancing girls'. All these and more could be enjoyed from the comfort of one's armchair. By 1860, the catalogue of the London Stereoscopic and Photographic Company already listed over 100,000 cards in stock.

It was photography that would give birth to the world of popular celebrity. In 1859, for example, Francis McClintock appeared as a returning hero to pose beside relics from the Franklin voyage. The following year Henry Maull released his book *Portraits of Living Celebrities,* a lavish album of photographs from his studio, shining the light on artists, bishops, assorted luminaries and landed gents. His five-shilling features of the famous had proven popular. The actor Charles Kean starred alongside the essayist Thomas Macaulay. The soon-to-be Prime Minister William Gladstone, stiff and uncomfortable, is out-performed by the missionary explorer David Livingstone, who appears in a bold pose clutching the horns of a rhino. In 1860, newspaper readers learnt of a new American invention that claimed to print over 12,000 stereographs per hour. This was a brave and brash new visual world.

Almost immediately after the invention of photography attempts were made to put the new technique to good use on explorations abroad. Little could the Swiss-born aristocrat Pierre Joly de Lotbinière have imagined what would follow him, when he sailed from Marseilles for the Middle East in 1839. He was the first to photograph the Parthenon in Athens and, travelling by donkey with more than 100 pounds of equipment

borne by camel, he later ventured along the Nile. Using exposures of 10 minutes or more in full daylight and, working in temperatures that made his thermometer explode, he managed to capture the magic of the Sphinx at Giza, the Pyramid of Cheops and Karnak Palace. When he returned to France, unsurprisingly, he was besieged by admirers. His photographs were a sensation.

By 1878, the Royal Geographical Society's *Hints to Travellers* offered advice to all would-be expedition photographers. Freed by the invention of dry plates, explorers could now penetrate mountain, river and jungle armed with the latest portable camera equipment. Of the old wet plate process, 'much practice and skill in manipulation is required in order to prepare photographic plates successfully, and this few travellers possess or can be expected to acquire', yet new technology 'has rendered it possible to take photographs anywhere and everywhere'. With their bulky cameras, boxes securely stocked with glass plates, camel's-hair brushes to combat desert dust, a copy of *Hints* possibly tucked in the pocket, and swathed in black velvet capes to block out the sun, a new breed of adventurous photographer stepped out into the unknown.

TO THE ARCTIC, WITH A CAMERA

Sir John Franklin's last expedition in 1845 was the first to take camera equipment into the Arctic, and so it is possible that the earliest photographic images of the polar regions were captured on this voyage. However, nothing survives. Like the ships and most of the men, there is, as yet, no

ABOVE: An intrepid 'camera-man on the wall of ice' in Peel Sound, 72°30'N, the first polar photographer to be featured as a portrait in the British newspapers, *The Illustrated London News,* 30 October 1875.

trace. Probably the earliest photographic images of the Arctic that have been found are calotypes by Dr William Domville of the *Resolute*, one of the many ships sent in search of the lost Franklin party.

This expedition left London in April 1852 and was the most ambitious of all the search campaigns. Again, a photographer from Beard's photographic establishment was there to capture portraits of the officers just before the five ships slipped down the Thames. Under the command of Captain Sir Edward Belcher, the squadron made its way to the north calling at Disko on the west coast of Greenland. There, sitting on a rock, a shipmate posed for Domville and the first photographic image was secured. Domville also tried to snap some Greenlanders but couldn't get his subjects to stay still: 'made an attempt to get the likeness of some of the natives with the Photography but could not succeed it being a matter of impossibility to keep them quiet, either laughing, talking or moving their heads at the most important moment of operation'.

Photographs, like popular lectures, poetry and art, all helped sustain an interest for exploration in the Arctic.

Much later in the voyage, Francis McClintock tried his hand at the new art but was similarly frustrated – 'I am practising with a calotype but am not very successful' – although he would capture a good shot of the ship *North Star* lying offshore in the ice of Erebus and Terror Bay, Beechey Island, shortly before she sailed for home. Under Domville's instruction, it appears McClintock gained in confidence. One shipmate recorded in his journal on 21 August 1854 that 'Capn McClintock after dinner taking likenesses on deck with a calotype'. Sadly, no examples of this pioneering photographic portraiture survive. On a later search voyage in *Fox* during 1857-59, McClintock took with him new equipment and also an official photographer, Dr David Walker, who doubled up as the ship's surgeon and naturalist.

When Captain Edward Inglefield set sail for the Canadian Arctic in the summer of 1854, *The Times* reported that he also took with him 'a most complete series of the articles used by photographists for depicting nature as seen in the polar regions'. Inglefield had admired the new wet-plate technique at London's Great Exhibition of 1851 and Archer's *Manual of the Collodion Photographic Process*, published the following year, was full of useful hints to encourage

the aspiring travel-photographer. In simple terms, the wet process involved a sheet of glass hand-coated with a thin film of collodion (guncotton dissolved in ether). It had to be sensitized and exposed while wet, and developed immediately, which meant all the chemicals and equipment had to be within easy reach. Though it was cumbersome, the technique produced images of quite breathtaking detail.

Inglefield was sent into Lancaster Sound on a cruise to make contact with Belcher's squadron. On the voyage north, ships often arrived at the Danish settlements in West Greenland, to take on extra supplies, to buy sledge dogs or engage local Inuit guides. As Inglefield's ship *Phoenix* called in at Holsteinborg, Disko, Jakobshavn and Upernavik, as well as a number of unpopulated fjords, it is difficult to identify all the harbours or portraits. Nevertheless, the photographs, of which 20 original glass negatives survive, offer a brief glimpse of life in the settlements of western Greenland during this time.

Inglefield was also a talented artist and he lectured a number of times with glass slides to help raise money for further searches: 'Inglefield begs away very handsomely', wrote Lady Jane to a friend. One of Franklin's nieces also attended an Inglefield lecture with her husband, the poet Alfred Tennyson. He 'was much interested and pleased'. Interestingly enough, the poet had wryly written that 'there is nothing worth living for but to have one's name inscribed in the Arctic chart', and Inglefield responded by naming Cape Tennyson on the north shore of Glacier Strait. At royal command, the explorer took many of his drawings to Windsor, and hung them in a corridor for the Queen to see after taking lunch. Photographs, like popular lectures, poetry and art, all helped sustain an interest for exploration in the Arctic; crucial if the cost of future voyages were to be justified by the Government or supported by the enthusiasm of public subscriptions.

In 1860, the American explorer Isaac Hayes produced the first multiple photographic prints of the Arctic. Having raised sufficient funds, Hayes purchased a schooner that he renamed *United States* and sailed from Boston for the west coast of Greenland on 12 August. He had just enough money for some apparatus – though not enough funds to recruit a photographer – so he settled to take the photographs himself. Just four days out of Upernavik, in waters choked with ice, Hayes had his first go at the travelling technique:

Practically, I knew nothing whatever of the art. It was a great disappointment to me that I could not secure for this expedition the services of a professional photographer; but this deficiency did not, I am happy to say, prevent me, in the end, from obtaining some views characteristic of the rugged beauties of the Arctic landscape. We had, however, only books to guide us. With our want of knowledge, and an uncomfortable temperature to contend with, we laboured under serious disadvantages.

By the end of his expedition Hayes had succeeded in taking at least 82 photographs, including views of the ship, scenery and portraits of native Greenlanders. Upon his return he made a quick profit by publishing them as both paper and glass stereoviews, and with this expedition it may be said that 'the use of photography as a means of documenting people, places, and events in the Arctic had come into its own'. Others were learning the art too. Another remarkable series of photographs – also of Greenlandic landscapes and settlements – were taken in Godthåb and Sukkertoppen between the years 1860 and 1865. Dr Hinrich Johannes Rink, a geographer and humanitarian, lived among the Inuit on the west coast for almost fifteen years. Many of his portraits were later reproduced in Denmark, featuring as a collage in some published works. Approximately 60 original photographs are known to survive. Later adventurers and explorers like Agnes Cameron, Philip Godsell and Vilhjalmur Stefansson continued to point their cameras at the region's indigenous people and never failed to include these photographs in their best-selling books and public talks.

This summary of Arctic photography could include many more eccentric individuals, such as the unfortunate Amos Bonsall, daguerreotype operator on Elisha Kent Kane's 1853 expedition, who left his photographs on a sledge that drifted away on an ice floe; the fur trader George Simpson McTavish; amateurs like James Cotte and Geraldine Moodie; the ethnologist Franz Boas, who lost most of his film on Baffin Island and faked a number of his photos in a studio back home in Germany; or Captain George Comer, the Hudson Bay whaler who astounded everyone, crew and natives alike, with his use of flash powder. Perhaps, remember George De Wilde, photographer on Allen Young's cruise in 1875, or the prolific William Grant, who also sailed with Young in 1876 and exhibited enlargements of his shots at the Photographic Society in London. Grant made another seven trips to photograph the Arctic,

producing a fascinating body of work that is still largely neglected by historians and anthropologists.

Nor must one forget the American artist William Bradford. Becoming obsessed with Arctic scenery, described so vividly by explorers such as Sir John Ross and Elisha Kent Kane, he made a series of pleasure cruises to Labrador, and felt compelled to travel to Greenland to observe personally 'the terrible aspects of the Frigid Zone'. In 1869, for his seventh and final Arctic expedition, he chartered a steamer named *Panther* and a crew of Newfoundlanders, and recruited Hayes as his companion. He also hired two Boston studio photographers, John Dunmore and George Critcherson, to join them. Bradford

ABOVE: Hinrich Rink's portrait survey of the Greenlandic Inuit, the first of its kind, 1865.

recognised the value of photography to capture images that he could later work with, creating his highly sought-after paintings. The two were voracious: taking shots up glaciers, under the midnight sun, dodging swarms of mosquitoes, and avoiding calving icebergs. They also secured a number of fine portraits. Proceeding northward into the ice, the adventurers were rewarded with their most exciting photographs yet. A mother polar bear and her two cubs were spotted and *Panther* gave chase:

> At this moment the photographers came rushing on the deck demanding the right of a 'first shot'. Quick as a flash the camera was down and focused, a slide with a little hole in it was dropped before the lens, and the family group of bears was taken at a distance of about two hundred yards. To accomplish this feat required the very first degree of enterprise and skill. The camera was stationed upon the top-gallant forecastle, and the impression was obtained while both ship and bears were in motion.

There was nothing romantic about what happened next. The bears were dispatched by rifle fire, and both hunters and prey were photographed in front of the ship. Bradford's account of the trip, *The Arctic Regions*, carried 141 original photographs, hand-pasted within the text and it was a prestigious success, with Queen Victoria first on its list of subscribers. Although only 350 copies of this huge elephant-folio were printed, it significance lies not only in that it was the first published work to include photographs of the polar regions, but also because of their range and quality and, interestingly, because a number of the photographs were manipulated, with figures drawn in, sometimes even ships inked onto the horizon. Elsewhere negatives were cropped, some artfully concocted as composite images, or embellished with dynamic skies.

Photographs became a sketchpad for grand compositions. It was from this material, as well as scores of oil sketches and drawings, that Bradford would work up in studios in New York, London and San Francisco the paintings for which he became famous. In commissioning a stunningly pink 'The Panther in Melville Bay', Princess Louise had selected her favourite photograph, on which Bradford then based his canvas. The photographs were also displayed as glass positives at the Somerville Gallery in New York, not hung like a conventional exhibition but, rather better, they were projected upon an enormous screen using a powerful lime light 'stereopticon' lantern. The voyage itself cost over $150,000 (Bradford's patron defaulted on the funding),

but its vibrant photographic and artistic output entitles it to a special place in this visual history.

Thirty years after Franklin, another British expedition sailed north under Captain George Strong Nares. Commanding the *Discovery* and the *Alert*, Nares steamed through the ice to Ellesmere Island, attaining a point farther north than any ship to date. From here man-hauled sledge parties were dispatched into the unknown: one east across Greenland; another west, and a third toward the Pole. The sledgers and many from the ships' company succumbed to scurvy, forcing the expedition to return a year early in 1876. Nares summed up the ordeal in a terse cable – NORTH POLE IMPRACTICABLE – a simple line that threatened to crush polar ambitions in a moment. However, the Arctic had lost none of its visual appeal and the public were gripped by the images of the heroic battle against an unforgiving wilderness.

By now the development of dry plate photography enabled pictures to be taken in intense cold. The pre-coated plates could be exposed some time after manufacture, and then developed later on board ship. Junior engineer of the *Alert*, George White, and Thomas Mitchell, the assistant paymaster of *Discovery* (later Paymaster-in-Chief of the Royal Navy), secured a series of stunning images. These photographs were crucial to the expedition's success. Borne home on the supply ship *Valorous*, some of the photographs were copied into lavishly engraved supplements in *The Graphic* and *The Illustrated London News*. Polar images featured almost on a weekly basis.

Meanwhile, in the Arctic, other members of the expedition were also having a go. For example, George Egerton, one of *Alert's* spring sledging party, tried his hand at the new technology:

> Never having taken a photograph in my life before, and having only had five minutes' instruction in the art, I was rather anxious to see what the result would turn out, so persuaded May and the crew to stand while I took a photograph of the camp, dogs and crew. I was some time getting ready, focusing, etc., and got very cold. When all was ready I took the cap off, out watch, and took the time – two minutes – May getting impatient – three minutes – I burst into a fit of laughter, as I suddenly remembered I had not drawn the slide off the plate. May was furious. After a great deal of persuasion I got them to stand again, and this time everything went off satisfactorily, except that I could not find the cap to put over the lens for some few moments …

RIGHT: William Bradford's *The Arctic Regions* was published in 1873. The following pages include its cover and some sample openings, one of which features his most popular image, 'Hunting by Steam'. Though only 350 copies of this huge elephant-folio were printed it was a sensation – it was the first book ever to include polar photographs.

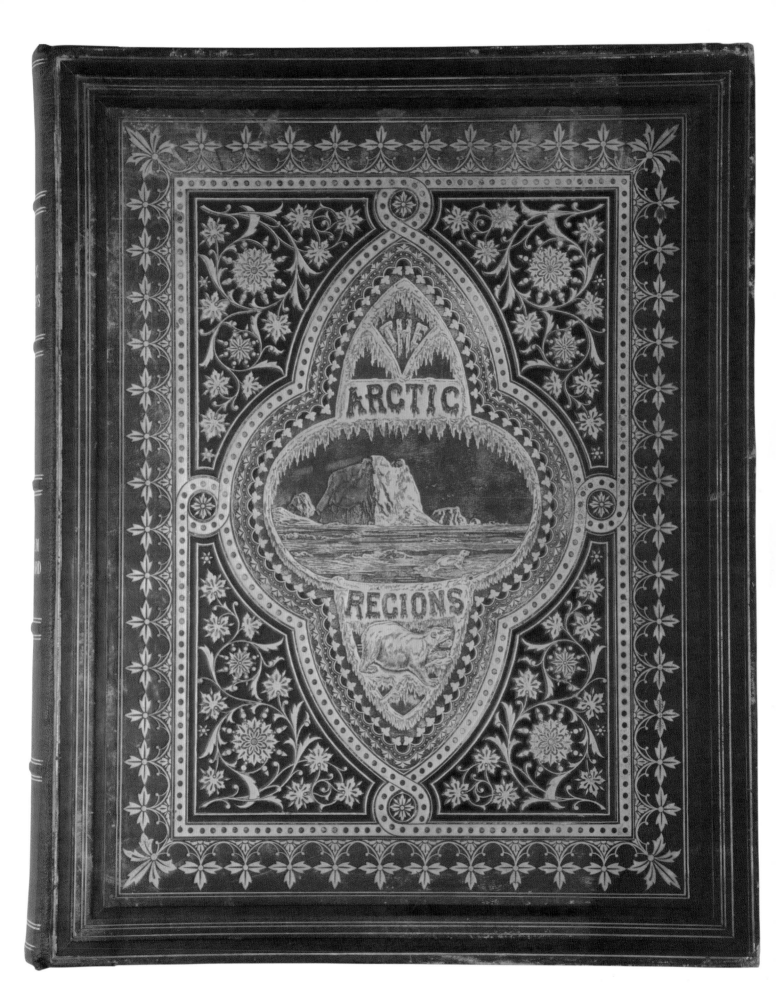

THE ARCTIC REGIONS

rapidly, but we were going three feet to his one, and overhauled him in proportion. When within less than a hundred yards, he disappeared around a projecting tongue of ice that we had not noticed, and the odds were again in his favour. Without a moment's hesitation the captain ran alongside of the floe, and, accompanied by some of the more enthusiastic huntsmen, scrambled down the side, started across towards the head of the

bight which the bear had entered, hoping to cut off his further retreat, but all too late. He was already out of the water, and making his way towards a line of hummocks which promised shelter. Volley after volley was sent after him without taking any effect, and, being much better fitted by nature for ice travel than were his pursuers, soon distanced them, and was lost to view. The party maintained the chase for half-an-hour or more, but were finally compelled to give it up, and returned aboard very much chap-fallen at the result. Bets were declared off, as was also the bear, and quiet reigned again in place of

No. 87.   The "Panther" trying to force a passage through the Floe.

the late enthusiastic excitement.

This lull did not last long, for the look-out man aloft again reported bears in sight away to the southward. Under his direction the "Panther" was kept away until they were visible from deck, when a plan for their capture was arranged. This chase did not prove a very exciting one, the ice being so weak and rotten that the bears (an old one again with two cubs), repeatedly broke through, thus leaving us to dispose of them at our pleasure. Seeing that they could not possibly escape, I restrained the impetuosity of our hunters until the photogra-

phers had with their usual skill and celerity taken an instantaneous view of the group. Then, starting ahead again, the bears were cut off from the main floe, and, being in the water, there was little difficulty in disposing of them. Hoisting them inboard, we kept away towards Wilcox Point, until a smooth place of solid ice was found. Into this we drove the "Panther," and, after she was snugly moored, the carcases were all lowered down over the side, and, being arranged in different positions, the hunters gathered around them, forming a novel and picturesque group, of which several views were taken.

The bears were then skinned and dressed, the choice portions of meat from the young and tender cubs hung up for future consumption, the skins given to those who were fortunate enough to establish a claim to them, and preparations made for another hunt if the opportunity presented itself.

No. 88.   In an open Lead between the Floe and Iceberg.

CHAPTER XIII.

Anchor under the Devil's Thumb—Dr. Hayes surveys the Devil's Thumb—Fine View from the top of the Mountain—Leave on
account of the dangerous position—Narrow Escape from being Nipped by the Ice-Floes.

S the ice opened on the ebb-tide, giving a clear lead in shore, we cast off from the floe, and working in past Wilcox Point, anchored about two and a-half miles from the Devil's Thumb. This was much nearer than vessels are accustomed to go, and the position was not without danger, on account of the strong eddies and currents which whirl around the bight, bringing in heavy floes and small bergs that would sweep any ship from her anchors and leave her wholly at the mercy of the pack.

Still, as my object was to obtain sketches and photographs of the most remarkable scenery on the coast, I resolved, notwithstanding the risk, to run in and accomplish all that we possibly could. Leaving the vessel with steam up, ready for an emergency, a large party of us landed and were soon scattered about as inclination or duty suggested.

Numerous traces of reindeer were discovered, some of them quite fresh, but none of the animals were visible, though it is probable we might have found them in large numbers had time permitted us to go a little distance up the fiord. On account of the dangerous situation of the "Panther," it was not deemed advisable to stray beyond the reach of signals, if she should be compelled to leave suddenly. For this same reason we gave our immediate attention to climbing the hill to the base of the "Thumb," which springs like a spire or tower to the height of about six hundred feet above the crest of the ridge, and is inaccessible to climbers at every point. By barometrical measurement we found the base of this pillar to be thirteen hundred feet above the level of the sea; adding to this the height of the Thumb proper, we have a total elevation of between nineteen hundred and two thousand feet.

So far as we could ascertain, the "Thumb" is situated on an island, six or seven miles long by four or five in width. We did not attempt to circumnavigate it, and I very much doubt the possibility of doing so, as the bay behind it and the passages on either side were choked up by innumerable floes and bergs which have been discharged from two great glaciers at the head of the bay. For this reason we could not assure ourselves that this was actually an island, but if it is not, the neck of land connecting it with the main must be very narrow.

From the elevation attained we had an unlimited view in all directions, and I was never before so thoroughly impressed with the idea of desolation. Immediately around, the soil, or rather the rocks, were unusually barren, even for these regions. To the southward and westward Wilcox Point projected its dark and gloomy form far nearly in line with the back, making her appear longer than she really was; lifting her feet stealthily like a cat, and putting them far out in front, as if feeling to make sure that the ice was strong enough to bear her weight. The cubs, on the contrary, gambolled around their dam, playing with each other like two kittens, rolling over and over, and splashing the water about in the many pools that had formed on the surface of the floe, totally unconscious of danger, and seeming to feel that everything was right so long as their mother showed no signs of alarm.

From their close proximity, I was enabled to sketch their natural movements upon their native ice, and I could not but note the different appearance they presented to the dirty, sleepy-looking animals of the same species that we see in menageries at home. The colour of the old bear's fur was a light yellow on the back and sides; the under portions and legs were of a more tawny hue, approaching a light brown, yet retaining a yellowish tinge, a long remove from the white colour generally attributed to the polar bear.

When within about seventy-five yards of us the old bear seemed to have her suspicions, for, stopping suddenly, she raised her head and snuffed the air in all directions; as if doubtful whether to advance or retreat. She finally compromised by moving around towards the "Panther's" stern, accompanied by the cubs, which kept up their fantastic gambols, though not straying far from her.

Fearing that they would get to the leeward and become alarmed by the scent from the vessel, I proceeded to rouse the sleepers, who at the word "Bears" came rushing on deck without regard to their toilets, and it was a task of some difficulty to keep them from alarming the animals, each being anxious to have the first shot. Captain Bartlett, with his long sealing gun, was first on deck, and by his exertions order was restored, and all heads kept below the rail, while preparations were being made for the chase.

The polar bear is proverbially cautious about approaching objects in motion, though anything of still life, unusual in appearance, will immediately attract his attention, and become a subject of close observation. At the sight or scent of man or dog, his fears are excited, and he will generally make off at full speed, without waiting to be attacked. Indeed, these animals are not the savage creatures they are generally supposed to be; and I do not know

No. 81. Instantaneous view of Polar Bears in the distance, taken while running over the Ice Floe.

of a single instance where they have been the aggressors. They are only dangerous when brought to bay.

Although our confusion soon subsided, there had been sufficient noise to alarm the mother, yet she was undecided in her motions. First advancing, then retreating, followed by the cubs, who began to partake of her anxiety, she worked gradually around to a long projecting spur of ice that extended some distance from the main floe nearly astern of us, evidently bent on satisfying her curiosity, though half inclined to run away. Had she pursued the latter course, there could have been no doubt of her escape, unless crippled by a chance shot, as the floe was wide, and in a race over it we stood a poor chance with the old bear, although the cubs might possibly have been overtaken.

Now, however, they were gradually working themselves into a trap, where there was little chance for them. The fires in the engine-room had only been banked; they were now opened to get up steam as quietly as possible. The lines were cast off, and as the bears ventured further on we backed easily, so as to bring the vessel's head to the southward. This alarmed the old bear, and with a sudden start she took the back track towards the main floe, while the cubs trotted after her, evidently partaking of her alarm, as their gambols stopped, and they floundered along, stumbling in the pools and losing valuable time. Had it not been for solicitude on her part for the cubs, the mother might easily have got away.

Full headway was given to the "Panther," and we shot towards what seemed to be the weakest portion of the spur, some distance inside of the bears' position. The crash was tremendous, but notwithstanding its severity everything kept its place, and the solid, iron-clad bows drove into the ice with sufficient force to open a lead

No. 13.—Hauling in the Manhaul Sledge. Crew in the background with ship in distance.

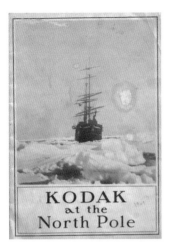

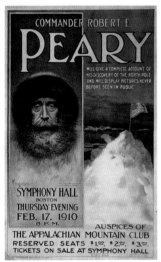

ABOVE: *Kodak at the North Pole*, the first manual for polar photography, endorsed by the explorer Robert Peary, 1893.

Poster advertising a Boston lecture by Peary in which he gave 'a complete account of his discovery of the North Pole', displaying photographs never before seen in public, 1910.

RIGHT: A collection of hand-painted glass magic lantern slides, used in public lectures to describe the perils and successes of the British Arctic Expedition under Sir George Strong Nares, 1875-76.

Despite official criticism, its leader Nares was welcomed home by an adoring crowd. His photographic portrait was engraved many times, and appeared on countless occasions in the new illustrated newspapers, often on the front page. His familiar image – broad brown whiskers, bald pate, stiff uniform, arms crossed in stern resolve – glowered from the covers of souvenir pamphlets, fold-out posters, and specially painted sets of magic lantern slides. However unremarkable an expedition and unromantic his professional appearance, his portrait as an explorer spread across the country with a quite remarkable speed.

Nares personally handled the publishing of the expedition photographs, too. Many of the images were truly excellent, fascinating shots, whilst the landscapes convey the vastness, isolation and austerity of the Arctic wilderness that few were able to describe as well in their written accounts. Countless 'photomechanical reproductions' were made for sale as prints, whilst the full set of 107 could be bought for a princely £10 14 shillings. One box, bound in red silk, was given to the Queen. She, no doubt, happily added these photographs to her growing collection.

PHOTOGRAPHY TRAVELS THE GLOBE

With the very successful use of cameras on this voyage, polar photography had come of age. Improvements in technology now meant that almost anyone with enough money could embrace this new visual world. The manufacture and marketing of dry plates and of developed printing papers increased substantially, costs were dropping, and more leisure time prompted a new hobby. The greatest change, however, was in camera design and in the materials the camera contained. With the introduction of the first 'Kodak' camera for sale in 1888, George Eastman set photography on a revolutionary course. In 1889, film as we know it today had been introduced. An early advertisement boasted 'Anybody can use the Kodak. The operation of making a picture consists simply of pressing a button. One hundred instantaneous pictures are made without re-loading. The operator need not learn anything about photography. *He can press the button - we do the rest*'. Of course, not all photographers wanted to hand the finishing work over to a factory, but what the mass-produced Kodak camera did achieve was to give the photographer a choice.

Robert Peary took advantage of new lightweight camera gear and, pleasing his sponsors, took many excellent photographs of the Arctic and its peoples. Based on his experiences he even wrote a do-it-yourself manual, *The Kodak at the North Pole*, certainly the first guide to polar photography. The Kodak Company printed it as a publicity piece and both explorer and business alike profited from this endorsement. At a more profound level, these technological advances made a huge change to the way people engaged with the world, and with those around them. Photography was instantly democratised. 'Anybody, man, woman or child, who has sufficient intelligence to point a box straight and press a button', could join in the fun.

The camera opened peoples' eyes to a world of new opportunity. It spelled escape, happiness, a land with wide horizons. In the same instant, it also set in motion the end of these sorts of freedoms. This new breed of 'snap-shot camera-man' multiplied almost overnight, joked *Punch* cartoonists. On lonely mountaintop or amidst the swirl of the summer party, 'the amateur photographic pest' was on hand to capture it all. Yet, little did people realise what they were about to sacrifice, entering this brazen new image-driven world. The pace of change was so quick that it would not be long before *paparazzi* appeared on the crowded streets.

For many explorers, however, photographers were not a nuisance, but a blessing. Exploration eagerly embraced this visual culture. In the field, an able photographer could capture an expedition's heroics in ways that were framed perfectly for its audience. Once home, a famous explorer would meet a legion of photographers hoping to secure a portrait, and the explorer was keen to strike the right pose. As now, a photograph could make, or break, a reputation.

Returning to London in the summer of 1909, Shackleton was greeted by a wave of celebration. His privately funded voyage on *Nimrod*, an expedition in which he toiled across the polar plateau to a record-breaking 'Farthest South' of 88°23', assumed the proportions of a national victory. Newspapers worked the public into a frenzy of adulation. In November, he was knighted in the King's Birthday Honours and he relished his moment in the spotlight.

More than any explorer before him, Shackleton's photographic image was everywhere. In private, like Scott, he was filled with self-doubt and anxiety, but in public certainly the outward figure he presented was simple – triumphant and courageous, the brave lion of the season. Crowds thronged the streets desperate for

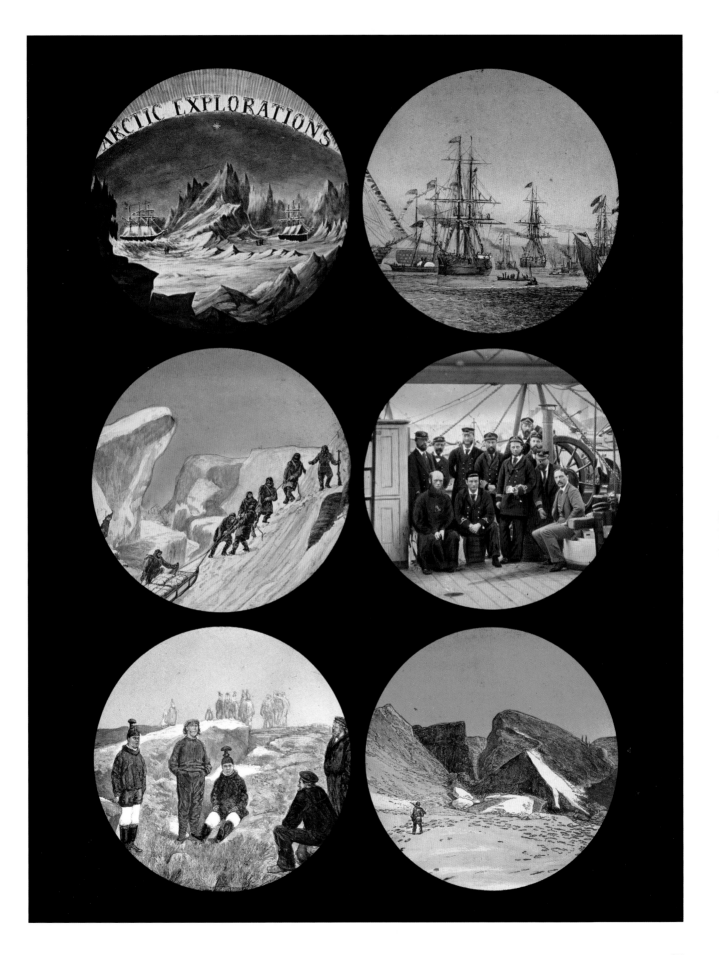

a glimpse of him. He tore round from civic receptions to gala dinners held in his honour and society hostesses vied for his presence at their fashionable gatherings. He became a model for the clothing company Burberry, he gave articles to magazines, endorsed products and accepted ovations across the country. He courted his public and they embraced him in return.

In the three years after his return from the *Nimrod* voyage, Shackleton gave hundreds of lectures. In order to turn his polar experience to greater profit, he created a new lecture, 'The South Pole', 'fully illustrated from Photographs and some very striking Kinematograph Films'. He went to great lengths to raise funds for what was to become the Imperial Trans-Antarctic Expedition, the most ambitious of all his many projects, which set out for the Antarctic, on the eve of the First World War, to cross the continent. Though many professional critics condemned his plans as ill considered and foolhardy, to large sections of the public for whom Shackleton had become the epitome of romance and daring, the very audacity of his project was appealing. The expedition, it is true, was a failure. But it was a *glorious* failure, made memorable for many by great personal achievements of courage, of endurance and of leadership: achievements of the kind that would give this era of polar exploration its familiar title, the 'Heroic Age'.

Shackleton travelled with his photographs all over Europe. In 1910, he embarked on a tour of the United States, where he met the other hero of the hour, Robert Peary, the man who claimed to have discovered the North Pole. Like Shackleton, Peary had also become master of the illustrated lecture, an ideal platform for maintaining and massaging his public profile. It was the power of the photograph, as much as their undoubted charisma, which fuelled this chaotic cycle of celebrity. They met again in 1913 in the company of the Norwegian explorer Amundsen – enjoying a lecture tour of his own – having bagged the South Pole on 14 December 1911.

One man's work as a polar photographer stands above all others. Herbert George Ponting was the official photographer on Scott's last expedition, which set out for the South in 1910. Ponting, who described himself as a camera artist, also took with him some of the first colour plates produced by the Lumière factory at Lyons. The expedition was certainly the best equipped, from the photographic standpoint, of any that had ever left England. The cameras for the sledging parties were specially made 'Sibyls' by Newman and Guardia,

166   PUNCH, OR THE LONDON CHARIVARI.   [OCTOBER 4, 1890.

THE AMATEUR PHOTOGRAPHIC PEST.

with attention paid to strength and compactness. The 'cinematograph' camera was built by Newman and Sinclair with unique Tessar lenses and pioneering 'reflex focussing' to ensure 'smooth running throughout'. The voyage south from Southampton was not so smooth, however. Scott wrote 'Ponting cannot face meals but sticks to his work constantly being sick … with a developing dish in one hand, and an ordinary basin in the other'. But his discomfort was soon repaid and, at the sight of icebergs, the photographer claimed that he was the happiest he had ever been in his life.

Conditions at base camp were predictably severe. Water froze in Ponting's tanks, flesh stuck to frozen metal and outdoor photography meant a constant risk of frostbite. Ponting continually badgered members of the team to appear in his photographs. It led to a new verb, to 'pont', meaning to 'pose until nearly frozen, in all sorts of uncomfortable positions', following

ABOVE: The new breed of 'snap-shot camera-man' could be seen everywhere, a cartoon from *Punch*, 1890.

LEFT: A full set of 107 photographs from the British Arctic Expedition, 1875-76, could be bought for the handsome price of £10 14 shillings. Featured here are: 'Group of Arctic Highlanders and Seamen of the Expedition at Cape York', 'Sledge Party Camped for Rest, on their journey to the North Coast of Greenland', 'Winter Quarters of the *Alert*, Mr White and Nelly, June 1876', 'Walrus Killed in Franklin Pearce Bay, 10 August 1875', 'Hans Henri, Esquimaux Dog-Driver, with his son and daughter', and 'Newly Formed Floe-Bergs, May 1876'.

Ernest Shackleton

much persuasion. Scott praised him many times in his personal journal: 'He is an artist in love with his work ... His results are wonderfully good, and if he is able to carry out the whole of his programme we shall have a photographic record which will be absolutely new in expeditionary work'. Ponting's cajoling of his messmates evidently worked and Scott was right to trust in his skill: he exposed around 25,000 feet of film and 2,000 photographic negatives during the expedition, capturing some of the most striking images ever obtained in the Antarctic. In their beauty and composition, they have rarely been equalled.

After the expedition's tragic outcome, Ponting lectured daily in London with a combination of film and slides. His photographs were first exhibited by the Fine Art Society at their fashionable gallery in New Bond Street and special copies, postcards and photographic portraits were sold widely. *Country Life* proclaimed his portraits the 'final perfection of the photographer's art', and many other magazines echoed in support:

When the wonderful technique of Mr Ponting's pictures is recognised, it is almost impossible to credit that these results were in many cases obtained under circumstances and difficulties seldom paralleled in the history of Photography... THE UNDYING STORY OF CAPTAIN SCOTT AND HIS FOUR COMRADES will always be an EPIC in the ANNALS OF EXPLORATION. It is A STORY OF DEVOTION TO PURPOSE, IDEALS AND DUTY, unparalleled in our time, and in no more popular way, perhaps, can its beauty better be realised than by means of these living pictures.

The future Prime Minister, Stanley Baldwin, was so impressed he ordered fifteen prints. The exhibition was later displayed in Scotland, Cambridge and Paris. *The Daily Mirror* urged that the photographs be shown in 'every picture palace in the kingdom'. Ponting also toured himself, lecturing, selling, exhibiting, even sending copies of the film and his photographs to troops on the Western Front. His celebrated lectures in 1914 at London's Philharmonic Hall were, by all accounts, a huge success too. Within two months he had performed over 100 times to an estimated audience of 120,000 people. 'Ponting's manner and delivery are excellent', noted Frank Hurley in his diary after seeing one of the shows, 'giving one the impression the penguins were actually performing to his words'.

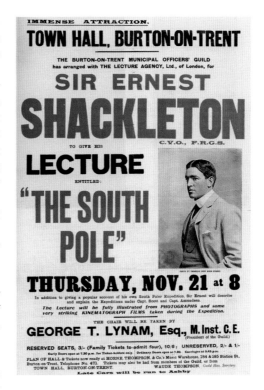

On 12 May, at a sparkling event at Buckingham Palace, he presented his photographs by royal command to a room filled with many of the crowned heads of Europe, including the King and Queen of Denmark. Newspapers echoed his fame, 'Mr Ponting has now succeeded in obtaining for photography all the acknowledgements which were reserved for drama, painting and literature'. His polar photographic portraits drew special praise. Ponting later wrote that King George 'told me that he hoped I should be able to deliver my Lecture throughout the provinces, as he thought that everyone, and more especially every British boy, should have knowledge of the Expedition'.

Though Ponting died in 1935, by his own account 'run down physically and cleaned out financially', his consolation lay in 'having loyally carried out a duty to the memory of those in the Barrier ice'. He devoted himself to preserving the record of the expedition and the memory of its leader who had meant so much to him. His film *With Captain Scott, RN, to the South Pole* remains a haunting classic and his photographs – now in the collections of the Scott Polar Research Institute – are an enduring visual memorial to the hardships and heroism of this Golden Age of Antarctic exploration.

LEFT: Sir Ernest Shackleton, more than any explorer before him, embraced photography as the key to his public fame. A selection of familiar and rare portraits. Among others, we see a young man with a floppy hat in 1907, a publicity shot for Burberry, weighed-down with medals in 1911, as a wax-work at Madame Tussauds, and waving a final farewell in 1921.

ABOVE: Shackleton's popular polar lecture 'fully illustrated with photographs and Kinematograph Films', delivered prior to announcing plans for his next ambitious expedition, which left for Antarctica in *Endurance* in 1914.

MOVING TO MOTION PICTURES

ABOVE: *Eskimo*, MGM's polar blockbuster, premiered at the Astor Theatre in Times Square, New York in 1933. The Inupiat actor Ray Mala became an international movie star.

RIGHT: A selection of ephemera from the SPRI collections. *The Daily Mirror*, for example, featured the first Ponting photographs to be seen by the public, sent to the newspapers during the fateful *Terra Nova* expedition, 1910-13.

Of course, it was the cinema that ultimately took the lead, surpassing the daguerreotype, the magic lantern, and the wet process photograph. Like the camera, the major difficulties were technical. To haul a motion-picture camera, developing equipment and a sufficient supply of film was a huge challenge soon made easier by improvements such as faster film and portable apparatus. Frank Hurley's pioneering 35mm footage, shot on Shackleton's attempt to cross Antarctica in 1914-16, is possibly the best of its kind. Of Hurley, the explorer Sir Douglas Mawson said: 'He is one of those to whom danger adds but a zest, one of those willing to undergo great hardships to accomplish an end'. In 1919, *Life Magazine* summed him up equally well: 'Hurley has youth, with youth's best qualities in singularly ample array – height, width, strength, and an irreproachable digestion; quickness, sure-footedness, level-headedness and an unfailing nerve; tireless energy and great elasticity. No wonder he can carry a camera around the world!'

Hurley's work, both photography and film, present a mix of dramatic polar portraits with landscapes of unprecedented beauty and ferocity. 'It may not be amiss', *Life Magazine* concluded, 'to point out here the important place that photography plays in modern exploration. The scientific discoveries – geographical, geological, biological – are more or less of a highly technical character; they are collected with meticulous care, and become the precious possession of the limited number of the scientific bent, who store them and use them in the cause of civilisation. But the photographer, if he possesses the mind of an artist, makes visible the work of all the scientists and for his own part translates to the world's people not the incidents of a single expedition merely, but the grandeur and the terror, the howling tempests, the aching silences – in short, the very soul – of the land'.

When *Endurance* sank, Hurley was able to save some of his glass-plate negatives, and an album of photographs he had already printed, now in the collections of the Scott Polar Research Institute.

He also managed to take 38 photographs with his small hand-held Vest Pocket Kodak after he was forced to abandon his equipment at Ocean Camp. The photographic portraits that survive from this expedition are all the stronger for their rarity. They open our eyes to exploration, as few others can. His work on the *Endurance* voyage stands as a lasting tribute to the courage of a small party of men who embarked on a voyage of discovery that turned into an epic struggle for survival.

Hurley's film was first shown as *South* in 1919, and was used frequently by Shackleton in his public lectures. It was also shown in Hurley's native Australia, where it was released to huge fanfare as *In the Grip of the Polar Pack Ice* in 1919, and it was later shown around the world. Other polar films followed, such as Robert Flaherty's *Nanook of the North*, which premiered in New York in 1922 as the first feature-length 'documentary'. Unduly criticised in recent years as over-romanticised, patronising, staged and inaccurate – it was all of these things – one must not forget *Nanook's* value as truly ground-breaking cinema. Technically innovative, Flaherty's filmmaking was way ahead of its time, and it provides portraits of people that can continue to tell us much in this changing, modern polar world. His sensitive photographs too, often overlooked, are also fine examples of his particular vision of the North.

Other explorers were realising the benefit of the multi-media approach, embracing both photographs and film to enhance the profile of their work. In 1932, for example, the Danish explorer Knud Rasmussen was a major contributor to the Universal Pictures production *SOS Eisberg*, the first feature film to be made in Greenland, and though not a box-office success, it did earn critical praise for the quality of its photography and for its evocation of the polar landscape. Friedrich Dalsheim's *The Wedding of Palo* (1934), for example, was made to raise funds for Rasmussen too, though he died just before the film's release. The year before, the Danish explorer Peter Freuchen collaborated with Hollywood filmmakers to produce the big-budget *Eskimo*, which despite moments of melodramatic inaccuracy remains in many ways one of the most authentic representations of Inuit life and hardship ever filmed.

For comparison one may also look to the work of Peter Pitseolak, whose photographs are well known, at least among the Inuit. He acquired his first camera – a fixed-focus Brownie – from a Catholic Priest in the 1940s and began taking candid portraits of his family in Cape Dorset. His photographs are unique, but he did not steer entirely clear of the nostalgia that affected Flaherty's work. Pitseolak preferred to depict people as they had lived in the past, taking care to photograph his friends in traditional clothing (one particular caribou parka and sealskin trousers went the rounds several times) and reconstructing hunting trips so he could record their fast-disappearing traditions. In the 1950s and 1960s, the distinguished art dealer Charles Gimpel, on the other hand, made six journeys to the Canadian Arctic and was quick to record a society in transition. He photographed the Inuit engaged in new activities such as mining, radio broadcasting, printmaking and racing their Ski-Doos, with as much care as he captured more traditional forms of living and working in the North.

There have been countless documentaries, photographic books, exhibitions and shows about the polar regions, its landscape and its people ever since. By 1968, the time of his last visit to the Arctic, the Inuit that Gimpel had come to know and love were beginning to be overwhelmed by such rapid social change and cultural dependency, that he found them almost unrecognisable. The modern Arctic is changing fast and it will not be long before much that is now familiar disappears from sight. With the release of *Atanarjuat* (2001), the first Inuit-written, directed and produced feature film, the polar portrait has dropped much of the baggage of the past, dumped many of the old visual clichés, and moved forward into a world of new possibilities.

Though cinema has swept all before it, the power of the photograph remains. Look closely at a historic portrait by Ponting and you are thrown immediately into the culture of exploration, you feel that you are *there*. Wrinkles are etched across weathered faces like glaciers inching their way down mountain valleys; makeshift snow-goggles, tattered hats and roughly-woven jumpers contrast with the elaborate gear of the modern explorer, yet there is something essential that unites the old with the new. These are the same people only dressed differently. The landscape of exploration has changed, but many of the same dangers, the same struggles and the same hopes remain. Their faces speak of adventure and ambition, sometimes of failure, and of dreams escaping into the wild, white spaces of the Poles.

Cambridge, 2008

POLAR PORTRAITS

In a multiplicity of ways, PHOTOGRAPHY has already added, and will increasingly tend to contribute, to the knowledge and happiness of mankind: by its means the aspect of our globe, from the tropics to the poles - its inhabitants, from the dusky Nubian to the pale Esquimaux, its productions, animal and vegetable, the aspect of its cities, the outline of its mountains, will be made familiar to us ... Amidst the icy barriers which have been placed to guard the hidden mysteries of the Poles, those who have had the daring to endeavour to penetrate their awful solitudes have made use of PHOTOGRAPHY to bring away the impress of them.   *MANUAL OF PHOTOGRAPHIC MANIPULATION, 1868*

If I could tell the story in words, I wouldn't need to lug a camera.

LEWIS HINE, 1932

GALLERY
POLAR PORTRAITS
HUW LEWIS-JONES

The collections held by the Scott Polar Research Institute, University of Cambridge, are among the richest in the world for the study of polar environments. Work began in 2007 on the FREEZE FRAME project to capture and preserve the archive of historical images in digital form.

The project aims to digitise over 20,000 photographic negatives from 1845, some of the very earliest imagery, through to the 1980s, representing some of the most important visual records of British and international polar exploration. This archive includes daguerreotypes, magic lantern slides, glass plate negatives and modern cellulose formats. Many of these images are unpublished, rediscovered within private albums and personal collections. Most have never been before the public eye.

Focussing on portraiture, FACE TO FACE draws attention to some of this recovered historic imagery, whilst looking to the contemporary polar world. The project engaged the leading expedition photographer Martin Hartley to add to his portfolio by producing a range of new commissions, featuring men and women of many nations, exploring, working and living in the polar regions today.

This is a gallery of 100 remarkable people; a photo album of travel and existence at the ends of our earth. This is neither complete nor definitive. Coming face to face with a selection of individuals in this way, we hope to recover and to celebrate the range of contributions within this modern landscape – and to reflect upon the memory and the legacies of exploration and survival in the polar world.

Cambridge, 2008

PREVIOUS PAGE:
Camera belonging to Sir Raymond Priestley, used in Antarctica on the *Terra Nova* expedition, 1910-13.

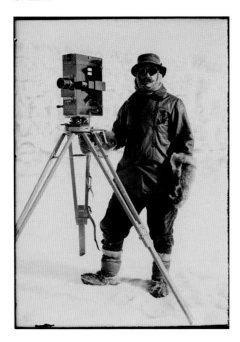

CAPE EVANS, 1912
HERBERT PONTING 1870-1935

Born in England, a Californian fruit farmer in his youth, Herbert George Ponting learnt his trade as a photographer on many travels in the Far East. By 1909, according to another polar photographer, he had become the 'best outdoor cameraman in the world'. Ponting journeyed south with Captain Scott and members of his 1910 British Antarctic Expedition. Scott described Ponting as 'an artist in love with his work', and after the expedition's tragic end Ponting devoted the rest of his life to ensuring that the heroism of Scott and his men would not be forgotten, immortalizing their noble failure.

An innovative photographer, Ponting was attracted to moving pictures too, adapting a Newman-Sinclair camera for the rigours of Antarctic use. Despite his inexperience he believed that 'the fascination of a moving, living picture is irresistible ... the cinematograph is undoubtedly one of the greatest educators of the century'. During the long polar winter he developed most of his breathtaking photographs and thousands of feet of film.

Ponting is posing with his cinematograph on 30 January 1912. 'The world of ours is a different one to him than it is to the rest of us', Scott wrote, 'he gauges it by its picturesqueness – his joy is to reproduce its pictures artistically, his grief to fail to do so ... he is enraptured and uses expressions which anyone else and alluding to any other subject might be deemed extravagant. Ponting is the most delighted of men; he declares this is the most beautiful spot he has ever seen and spends all day and most of the night in what he calls "gathering it in" with camera and cinematograph'.

ITALIAN ALPS, 2005
SIR RANULPH FIENNES 1944-

Sir Ranulph Fiennes is described as 'the world's greatest living explorer' by the *Guinness Book of Records* and his achievements prove this is no exaggeration. He was the first man to reach both Poles by surface travel and the first to cross the Antarctic Continent unsupported. He is the only person yet to have been awarded two clasps to the Polar Medal for both the Antarctic and the Arctic Regions. Fiennes has led over 30 expeditions, including the first polar circumnavigation of the Earth.

Ranulph Twisleton-Wykeham-Fiennes, known as 'Ran' to his many friends, inherited a baronetcy after the death of his father, a Lieutenant-Colonel, in action at Monte Cassino in 1943. He was educated at Eton and later joined his father's cavalry regiment – the Royal Scots Greys – before being seconded to the SAS. After numerous escapades, and becoming disillusioned by his British Army service, Fiennes turned his attention to exploration and adventure. In recent years, he has combined a career as a best-selling author and public speaker, with wide fundraising activity. His support for Marie Curie Cancer Care, for example, is likely to raise over £3 million and he continues to be an inspiration to a global audience.

This portrait was captured as Fiennes was training for a climb of the Eiger, a five-day ascent of the North Face, which he successfully completed in 2007. Martin Hartley joined him to secure some photographs for US magazine *Men's Journal*, who were running a feature on the explorer's heroics. That day, Fiennes headed off on a multi-pitch climb up a frozen waterfall, whilst Hartley circled round to the top to get a good shot. Fiennes later emerged – his face covered in blood, hit by a piece of falling ice – bothered only by the thought that he may have missed lunch.

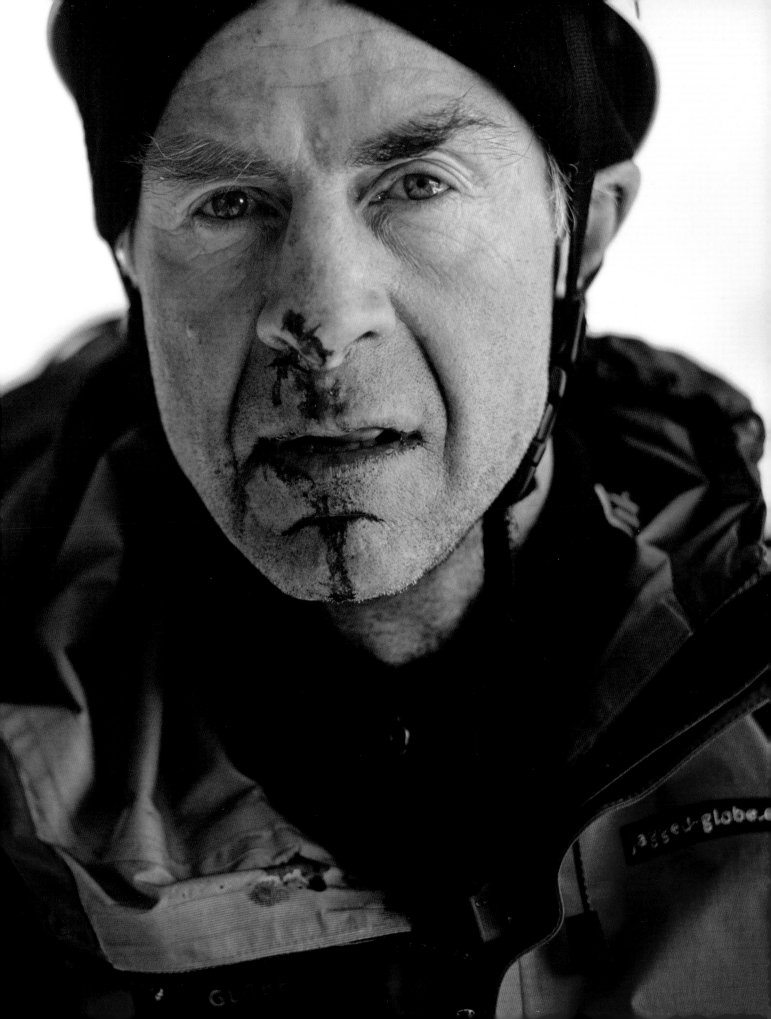

DUNDEE, 1886

URIO ETWANGO 1859-n.d.

Urio Etwango, a Greenlandic Inuk, was brought to Dundee in 1886 by Captain William Adams of the whaling steamer *Maud*. This studio portrait served as a publicity photograph to advertise a show that had been arranged whilst Etwango was in Scotland. He wintered in Dundee and returned to the Arctic in 1887. On the way home Etwango visited Lerwick, where on 16 March 1887 he demonstrated his kayak in the harbour before a large crowd of Shetlanders.

It is clear that Etwango was a willing participant in this trip from the Arctic, but the history of British exploration in the North has countless episodes of encounters and exploitation of indigenous peoples. Martin Frobisher brought three Inuit hostages to Bristol in 1577. The Inuit Tookoolito, Ebierbing and the young boy Haralukjoe were brought to England in 1853 where they were presented to Queen Victoria at Windsor Castle. In 1824, a semiliterate Yankee whaler by the name of Samuel Hadlock Jr brought two 'Esquimaux' from Baffin Island and displayed them as trophies among a variety of polar artefacts at the Egyptian Hall in London. Business was slow in the capital, so he turned to the provinces and then Europe. Hadlock was later lost while on a sealing expedition in the sordid search for new exhibition material.

Most Scottish ports, particularly those on the east coast such as Peterhead and Dundee, began whaling in the early 1750s and the trade thrived to become a successful industry. Whale blubber was made into oil that was, long into the nineteenth century, used to light the streets of Britain's rapidly expanding cities. By the 1890s, Dundee was the only port still operating whalers and in 1892 company owners turned their attention south and sent a whaling expedition to the Antarctic. It was the prowess of the Scottish whalers in ice conditions and their skills in ship construction that led Captain Robert Scott to Dundee. *Discovery* was launched into the Tay, in suitably snowy conditions, in 1901. Scott also used the veteran whaling barque *Terra Nova* for his second voyage in 1910.

GJOA HAVEN, 2003
INUIT GIRL 1995-

This portrait was taken on 1 April 2003 during the Hamlet Day celebrations in the Bay of Gjoa Haven (Uqsuqtuuq), King William Island. Hamlet Day is a national holiday when the whole village takes part in an Inuit version of the Winter Olympics. Snowmobiles are raced around a circuit. This young girl, dressed in her traditional furs, was taking part in a treasure hunt, looking for money buried in the snow (in white envelopes). The next day an announcement came over the local radio urging everyone to keep up the search – none of the buried money had been found!

In 1903, the Norwegian explorer Roald Amundsen was attempting the first navigation of a northwest passage. By October, the straits through which he was travelling began to ice up and he put his ship *Gjøa* into a natural harbour on the southeast coast of King William Island. They stayed there for nearly two years, in what Amundsen called 'the finest little harbor in the world'. He spent that time with the local Netsilik Inuit, learning to live off the land and travel efficiently. This knowledge proved to be vital for his later successful expedition to the South Pole. He explored the Boothia Peninsula, searching for the exact location of the North Magnetic Pole. Many of the present Inuit claim to be descendants of Amundsen and his crew.

NEW YORK, 1924
ROALD AMUNDSEN 1872-1928

When the young Roald Engelbregt Gravning Amundsen was still a boy he read the journals of Sir John Franklin. As he later wrote, '... they thrilled me as nothing I have ever read before. What appealed to me most were the sufferings that Sir John and his men had to endure. A strange ambition burned within me, to endure the same privations ... I decided to be an explorer'. He followed this dream with a dedication that verged on obsession, turning polar exploration into an extraordinary career.

Between 1903-06 he sailed the tiny smack *Gjøa* through a northwest passage, completing Franklin's goal. He later turned his attention toward the Antarctic. For Amundsen, photography was not an art, merely a method for recording and a means to illustrate his talks at home. In fact, photographs were doubly essential to his public performances when he travelled out of his native Norway. Apparently his accent was so 'indescribable' that audiences in England and America often ignored his lecturing altogether, preferring instead to concentrate on his unusual slides.

Before his triumphant expedition to the South Pole, Amundsen had one of Norway's famous professional photographers, Anders Beer Wilse, instruct his men in shooting and developing film in an effort to improve the trip's visual record. Wilse, however, was not impressed: 'But Amundsen himself would not have any lessons. He had a normal Kodak 6 x 9. If I take six pictures with different openings and times, then one of them must be usable, he said. But he lost many thousand kroners income, because he did not have proper pictures when he came home. I remember I worked hard to make proper slides for his lectures from the hopeless amateur material he had produced'.

This rare studio portrait from 1924 was taken when Amundsen was in New York to begin a new lecture tour, sorely lacking funds for his next venture. He may not have had the best photographs in the world, nor the patter with which to enthrall an audience, but for his achievements in exploration alone Amundsen stands without equal. In 1911 he snatched the South Pole from Scott's grasp. In 1926, aboard an Italian Zeppelin piloted by Umberto Nobile, he flew over the North Pole.

RESOLUTE BAY, 2007
PAUL IKUALLAQ 1955-

Paul Ikuallaq was photographed at South Camp Inn, Resolute Bay. Hartley met him when he was on assignment in the Arctic, photographing the English adventurer Rosie Stancer's preparations for her North Pole Solo expedition in 2007. Paul claims to be a grandson of the Norwegian explorer Roald Amundsen who overwintered in the area during his navigation of a northwest passage in 1903-06.

Ikuallaq runs a Bed and Breakfast business in Gjoa Haven, but on this occasion he had been drafted over to Resolute Bay to help build 55 dog sleds for the Canadian Rangers, who were planning a huge expedition across Ellesmere Island in an attempt to further establish sovereignty in the area.

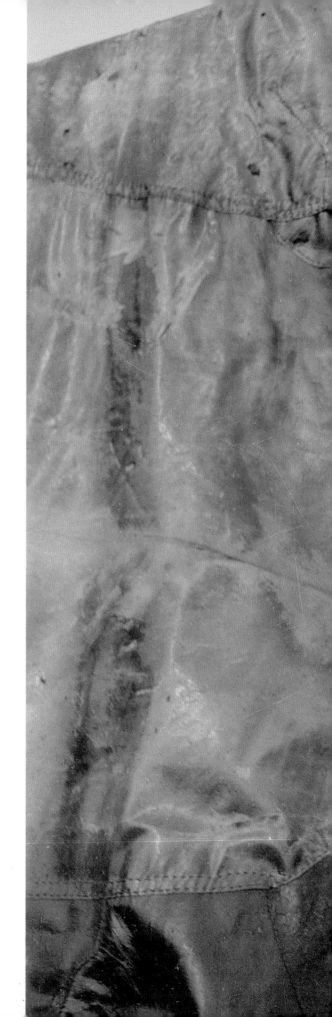

NETTUI, 1930
POTARDINA AND CHILD 1898-n.d.

This portrait is part of an unpublished series of photographs taken by Spencer Chapman, near Angmagssalik on the east coast of Greenland, during the British Arctic Air Route Expedition of 1930-31 led by George 'Gino' Watkins. At that time there were about 700 Inuit living within 50 miles to the north and south of the settlement, in addition to the Danish magistrate-cum-storekeeper, a wireless operator, a half-Inuk missionary and their families. This is probably a widow called Potardina from the camp at Nettui, with an orphan she had adopted, standing before their sealskin tent.

Chapman was the expedition's ornithologist. Over the course of the trip he conducted an impressive field survey of bird species, including Purple Sandpiper, Golden Plover, Greenland Mallard, Ivory Gull, Snow Bunting and Arctic Tern. After their return to England in 1931, Gino's time was consumed with the planning of a new expedition to cross Antarctica and the onerous task of writing the official account fell to Chapman.

He wrote candidly about his interest in the local women. Overwintering a short distance across the fjord from Angmagssalik, the expedition set up its base hut 'like a well-organised country manor' and installed a household staff of four Inuit in the attic. One pretty woman in particular – Potardina's daughter, known as 'Gertrude' – attracted the attention of the young men, despite her almost constant hysteria. She was soon fired for refusing to do any work at all, other than regularly throwing cups and saucers out of the window.

IQALUIT, 2005
MATTY MCNAIR 1958-

Matty McNair was born in Pennsylvania, but now lives in Iqaluit, Baffin Island, where she runs her polar travel company NorthWinds. After a 22-year involvement with the Outward Bound schools across North America, McNair turned her attentions to polar travel. In 1990, she covered 4,000km around Baffin Island by dog sled. In 1997, she led the first ever all-female expedition to the North Pole and later led two ski-all-the-way expeditions to the South Pole. In 2003, she crossed the Greenland Ice Cap with her children, using ski-kites with dogsled support and, in 2005, led her children on an unsupported expedition to the South Pole. The team kite-skied back in a record breaking 17 days. In one day they covered 107 nautical miles.

McNair's portrait was captured in February 2005, shortly before she guided a team of British amateurs along Peary's 1909 route to the North Pole. This expedition garnered some press coverage in Britain, but little attention was paid to McNair, its leader, without whom the men on the trip would have had little hope of surviving on the ice, let alone reaching their goals.

'Possibly one of the toughest people you'll ever meet, a lovely woman', said one of her clients, McNair's achievements as a polar guide are matched by only by a select few. When not off on adventures freezing her nose and toes, she enjoys reading a good book in a rocking chair with a strong cup of coffee. She throws earthenware pots in her ceramic studio, designs and makes outdoor equipment (from tents to Arctic boots), paints in watercolour and plays with the Iqaluit fiddle group.

LONDON, 1845
SIR JOHN FRANKLIN 1786-1847

Franklin was suffering from a severe bout of 'flu when this picture was taken. He was 58 years old, a famous man after a long-serving naval career. It is 1845, the dawn of the photographic era. He wears the undress uniform of a Captain of the Royal Navy, with three large buttons on his cuffs, and a *chapeau* (cocked hat) of black silk. Perched on his shoulders, his gold epaulettes have an anchor on the strap and are surmounted by a crown. Pinned proudly to his chest is the star of the Most Honourable Order of the Bath and the Knight of the Order of the Redeemer of Greece. He holds a telescope to strike a bold pose as the leader of the new Arctic expedition. It was his first ever photograph and it was the last the public would see of him. His ships sailed from the Thames on 19 May 1845 and were lost without a trace.

Over thirty search expeditions were sent out in an effort to find them. An obituary notice, in 1856, remarked, 'His memory will ever be enshrined on British land within British hearts, as an explorer as eminent in discovery, as he was patient under trial and privation, and kind and good in all the relations of life'. Around his neck Sir John wears the insignia of the Knight Commander of the Royal Hanoverian Guelphic Order, which he received in 1836. Amazingly, it was found in the Arctic by the explorer John Rae at Repulse Bay in 1854; one of the few relics to survive, but of the ships and most of the men there is still no sign. In the intervening years rumours of madness, starvation and cannibalism shocked the British public, yet even today this polar tragedy attracts newspaper attention the world over.

In the 1980s the frozen bodies of three of the crew were found in an ice-filled grave. In 2008, the Canadian Government announced a new search effort involving a Coast Guard icebreaker using sonar equipment to survey an area of the seabed south of King William Island. The initial search will last six weeks, followed by further explorations in 2009 and 2010, if needed. In the face of geopolitical competition, Canada is asserting its sovereignty over the Arctic in a variety of ways – historically, militarily and environmentally. Prime Minister Stephen Harper declared that 'to protect the North, we must control the North'. As global warming shrinks the Arctic sea ice, Russia, the US, Canada and other nations are staking claims to areas potentially rich in gas and oil. The search for a lost expedition plays out amidst a great scramble for resources in the North.

PATRIOT HILLS, 2006
DAVID DE ROTHSCHILD 1978-

In 2005 David de Rothschild founded Adventure Ecology, an organisation that uses adventure and storytelling to captivate the imagination, raise global mass media awareness and inspire individuals, communities and industry to take positive action for our planet. His commitment to the environment has sent him on adventures to some of the world's most remote and fragile regions. In 2006, Rothschild organized an expedition to cross the Arctic from Russia to Canada. He has also participated on a traverse of Antarctica and was part of a team that broke a record for a speed crossing of the Greenland Ice Cap. In 2007, *GQ* magazine named him 'Environmentalist of the Year'.

This portrait was taken in Antarctica on a training day in Patriot Hills. 'It wasn't that cold, but the wind was cutting through the insulation of our clothing like a knife so we had to keep our faces totally covered', he says. Rothschild was part of a four-man team that was about to depart for the Ross Ice Shelf on a trans-Antarctic crossing, up the Axel Heiberg Glacier and across the South Pole.

In December 2008, Rothschild and a crew of experts, creative partners and scientists will sail 8,000 miles across the Pacific Ocean from San Francisco to Sydney in a boat made out of plastic bottles and recycled waste products. This voyage is named 'The Plastiki', taking inspiration from Thor Heyerdahl's epic 1947 expedition in *Kon-Tiki*. Rothschild hopes this adventure will captivate the public imagination by championing sustainable design and by telling the story of our oceans and the many challenges the world's inhabitants face.

MAUDHEIM, 1951
JOHN GIÆVER 1901-1970

John Schjelderup Giæver was leader of the wintering party of the Norwegian-British-Swedish Antarctic Expedition, 1949-52. This portrait was taken at their base, Maudheim, by second-in-command Valter Schytt, on his portable Hasselblad camera. The Norwegian-British-Swedish Expedition helped draw to a close the series of competing national expeditions that characterised the Heroic Age of Antarctic exploration. It ushered in an era of international cooperation and scientific collaboration that continues to this day.

The expedition was a huge scientific success, though not without considerable challenges for its leader. It took the party some weeks to recover from their shock and despondency at the death of three companions, drowned in a tragic accident. Giæver kept his men together, later writing 'Life must keep its course and be carried on, even where death has taken its toll. The war had taught us that'.

Norwegian-born, Giæver started his career as a journalist, before turning his hand to polar game hunting. He was leader of an expedition to Northeast Greenland in 1932-34 and, from 1935, served as secretary to the Norwegian research expeditions in Svalbard and the Arctic. After variously serving during the Second World War as aircraftsman and civil affairs diplomat, he turned his attention to the polar regions. He was office manager at the Norsk Polarinstitutt until 1960 and garnered acclaim over the years with his numerous books on Arctic trapping, welfare, fishing and exploration. The polar scientist, Charles Swithinbank, recalls meeting him for the first time: 'He was tall, handsome, and had a commanding presence. He kept a ready smile and I liked him at once'.

ESSEX, 2006
ROSIE STANCER 1960-

Described by Martin Hartley as a mix of 'Tinkerbell and Terminator', a comment that still raises a smile across her beautiful face, Stancer is not a typical polar explorer. She's just 5ft 3in and weighs eight and a half stone, yet is stronger and more determined than most men. Stancer has been photographed training at her home in Essex in 2006, preparing for her solo attempt on the North Pole the following year.

Over 10 years ago, Stancer joined an all-female relay trek to the North Pole. 'It was like a lit match being dropped on petrol', she says. 'The moment I stepped foot on polar ice, it confirmed that passion'. Since then she has turned herself from an amateur into an elite polar athlete, whilst also keeping-up with the demands of motherhood, an inspiration in itself. Stancer is also a director for the charity Special Olympics GB, which provides sports training and competition events for people with learning disabilities.

Her grandfather, the Earl Granville, intended to join Scott's fateful *Terra Nova* expedition but was told that, at 6ft 4in, he was too tall for the tents and would require extra rations. Stancer's immediate family is supportive, particularly her husband, grandson of Sir James Wordie, geologist on Shackleton's *Endurance* expedition. The face of exploration has changed in recent decades, with women often leading the new generation of adventure-athletes. The key, Stancer says, is not to suffer like the men: 'You get all these stories from traditional polar types of staggering and starving and conquering. But if you take it at a more gentle, intuitive pace, you enjoy the journey'.

LONDON, 1909
ROBERT FALCON SCOTT 1868-1912

An unremarkable torpedo officer, plucked from obscurity in 1901 to lead the first British Antarctic expedition for over fifty years, Robert Falcon Scott was not obsessed with the polar regions, unlike so many of those who travelled with him. He was honest enough to admit that he only began reading polar books a few months before he left for the South. Though unable to reach the Pole, the *Discovery* expedition, 1901-04, was a huge success, making valuable contributions to the knowledge of Antarctica and, on its return, Scott was promoted to a Captaincy in the Navy.

Scott appears here in 1909, shortly before the birth of his only child, Peter Markham Scott. This photographic portrait, quite unlike the heroic portraits we so often see of him, presents the explorer in a tender pose. Scott was a great reader and lover of good literature; his books, *The Voyage of the Discovery* and *Scott's Last Expedition* – the diary of the great adventure to which he gave his life – demonstrate his ability as a writer.

Though Scott reached the South Pole on his second expedition, in January 1912, he was beaten by his Norwegian rival Roald Amundsen, who had raced there using dogs and skis. Scott and his party perished on the return journey. Elevated to the status of a martyr by the public at home, Scott's achievements as an explorer have been unfairly questioned in recent years. He was a tough and capable leader – as well as a sensitive and affectionate husband – and reading his journals one cannot help but admire him.

The Scott Polar Research Institute was founded in 1920 as a lasting memorial to his polar work and to the contributions of those who served alongside him. It is fitting that it houses the world's finest polar library and archive whilst also leading in the field of polar science. Its museum, which now holds much of his equipment and diaries, opened in 1934 with the words 'Quaesivit arcana poli videt dei', inscribed in stone above its doorway: 'He sought the secret of the pole but found the hidden face of God'.

PUNTA ARENAS, 2003
SIMON MURRAY 1940-

In February 2004, the British adventurer Pen Hadow guided Simon Murray on a 680-mile trek in Antarctica – enabling Murray, at 63 years, to become the oldest person by a decade to reach the South Pole. The previous record holder was Sir Ranulph Fiennes, who was a decade younger when he made his successful crossing of Antarctica in 1993. Murray's expedition raised over £250,000 in support of the archives of the Royal Geographical Society. Murray's portrait is captured in a café in Punta Arenas, Chile; the same one in which Shackleton is said to have dined after he returned from the *Endurance* epic. It was the fourth time his flight to Patriot Hills had been cancelled so, dressed in full Antarctic clothing, he left the airport and headed straight to the nearest place for food and beer.

Born in Leicester, Murray was educated at Bedford School and as a teenager he worked his way to South America in the ship's galley of a tramp steamer. Murray is the author of *Legionnaire*, a best-selling book that detailed the unremittingly harsh regime of life in the French Foreign Legion. He joined as a young man in 1960 and spent the next five years in Algeria with its Parachute Regiment, enduring endless marches and skirmishes with the Algerian Fellegah in the Atlas mountains. Murray is described by Martin Hartley as 'very generous, very funny and very, very hard'. They first met in a tent, 30 miles offshore Resolute Bay, floating on the Arctic pack. It was one of the coldest days on record.

For nearly 40 years, Simon Murray CBE has enjoyed a successful business career in Asia, including time as Executive Chairman of the Asia Pacific division of Deutsche Bank. He currently runs his private equity fund management business based in Hong Kong and serves on the boards of a number of international companies. He shares his passion for adventure with his wife Jennifer, the first woman to fly solo round the world in a helicopter.

MAUDHEIM, 1951

BJARNE LORENTZEN 1900- n.d.

Lorentzen was 'a cheerful, wizened little man' from Lödingen, northern Norway. Born in 1900, he had spent most of his life at sea in overseas trade and the whaling industry. He joined the Norwegian-British-Swedish Antarctic Expedition of 1949-52, during the second year of its operations, as the replacement cook. This portrait was taken at Maudheim Base by second-in-command Stig Valter Schytt, taken on his portable Hasselblad camera.

Lorentzen was well-liked by the expedition's diverse team, for his attention to detail and general bonhomie. He had brought with him a year's supply of newspapers, which he had collected up to the day the ship *Norsel* left Oslo, bearing him to the Antarctic. Throughout the winter, Lorentzen placed a daily newspaper on the breakfast table. Although exactly one year out of date, this small gesture made a huge impact on the lives and morale of the men.

Spontaneous concerts were held from time to time and Lorentzen strummed along on an instrument he had fashioned from a broomstick, an empty food tin and a piece of wire. On 17 May, Norway's national day, he prepared a feast for the men: soup, smoked salmon, smoked mackerel, silverside, roast chicken with roast potatoes and fried mushrooms, followed by an enormous sponge cake covered with thick whipped cream and generous servings of punch, port, whisky and Guinness. Unfailingly cheerful throughout the long polar winter - even telling the men he had 'never been so happy in all his life' – they later discovered one element to his happiness: he had taken to sampling aquavit from a store box stashed outside.

RESOLUTE BAY, 2008
RANDY REID 1954-

Tired of Barbados, Randy headed north in 1998 to work on a temporary contract and he has been in the Arctic ever since. He is now chef at the South Camp Inn, a hotel in Resolute Bay. His boss, Aziz 'Ozzie' Kheraj, came to Canada in 1974 from Tanzania. He also moved north in search of work, first as a mechanic, and soon started his own construction business.

Kheraj opened South Camp Inn in 1998. His hotel now offers rooms complete with Jacuzzi tubs and Internet to customers who visit from all over the world. A satisfied customer described Randy's skills as a chef: 'Man, he's the perfect polar re-fueller ... his main job is making travellers fat before they set off across the ice ... and he does a great job of that!' In the Arctic, it is said, Randy's muffins are legendary.

SOUTH ATLANTIC, 1908
SIR ERNEST SHACKLETON 1874-1922

Born in 1874 in County Kildare, Ernest Henry Shackleton first visited Antarctica in 1901-04 with Scott and then led the first of his own expeditions in 1907-09. When this photograph was taken he was at sea, eating a snack on deck of his ship *Nimrod*. Relaxed, away from the pressures of home, Shackleton was in his element. It was a hugely successful expedition, reaching the South Magnetic Pole, achieving the first ascent of the volcano Mt Erebus and a march by Shackleton that came within 100 miles of the Pole itself. He returned home to huge fanfare.

When Amundsen announced his conquest of the Pole in 1912, Shackleton turned his attention to another challenge, writing: 'There remained but one great main object of Antarctic journeyings – the crossing of the South Polar continent from sea to sea'. The result was the Imperial Trans-Antarctic Expedition of 1914, aboard *Endurance*; a pioneering voyage that become an epic of survival. His ship was crushed, forcing his men to take to the ice before reaching a remote lump of rock called Elephant Island, from where he embarked on the 800-mile journey to South Georgia in an open boat to find help. Not a single man was lost.

Undoubtedly a great leader – known as 'The Boss', and beloved by his men – Shackleton's ambition was unrelenting. The years had taken their toll. After the First World War, joined by many who had served with him on previous adventures, he led a final expedition to Antarctica. He died in 1922 of heart failure and was buried by his shipmates at the South Georgia whaling station of Grytviken. When asked about polar leadership, one companion vividly described the strength of the man: 'Scott for scientific method, Amundsen for speed and efficiency but when disaster strikes and all hope is gone, get down on your knees and pray for Shackleton'.

SIBERIA, 2004
VALERIA BORRAJO 1973-

Valeria Borrajo travelled to Siberia to bid farewell to her boyfriend, the young British adventurer Ben Saunders, as he attempted a solo and unsupported crossing of the Arctic Ocean. On this morning in 2004, Saunders was training, skiing up the frozen Khatanga River and testing his kit. The weather had not risen above −43°C during the previous ten days.

Khatanga is a village in the Taymyr Peninsula, on the edge of the Arctic Ocean. It is one of the most northerly habitations in Russia. The area is often visited by Western tourists as an entry point into the Siberian wilderness, and also used as a base by aspiring polar adventurers looking to the North Pole. Born in Granada, southern Spain, Valeria was not so impressed by the formidable cold. Asked about exhibiting this portrait, she was beautifully relaxed: 'I suppose freezing all morning did pay after all! I really don't know what to say about me since I do not have any expeditions 'under my belt'. Oh well, *hasta luego*!'

'For someone born in sunny Granada', she later told us, 'Siberia doesn't seem like the obvious place to end up. However, I am convinced that every place holds an unexpected side and Khatanga proved no different. My first impression was that of the aftermath of a nuclear explosion. For a town of 3,000 people, things seemed pretty dead, but being stranded there for a fortnight at the mercy of Russian bureaucracy gave me the opportunity to discover a different side to the city. I discovered that life quite literally goes on behind closed doors. Shopping for supplies meant trying the town's blank and nameless doors at random. Opening them one by one revealed a grocery shop, a ladies' lingerie boutique, a bar and even a store selling the latest hits at that latitude. I guess even the bitterest cold can't stop a dedicated *Granadina* from eventually hitting the shops'.

ANGMAGSSALIK, 1930
INUIT WOMAN 1901-n.d.

This portrait is part of an unpublished series of beautiful photographs taken by Alfred Stephenson in the summer of 1930, during the British Arctic Air Route Expedition led by George 'Gino' Watkins. Stephenson was given the role of chief surveyor, despite having only finished his final Tripos exams barely three weeks before the expedition sailed from London. Early on the morning of 24 July the *Quest* reached Angmagssalik on the east coast of Greenland where they were met in its ice-scattered approaches by a crowd of some 100 Inuit locals.

Spencer Chapman, the expedition's young ornithologist, was amazed by their welcome, and particularly taken by the women who clambered aboard. 'The Danish Government ship only visits the settlement once a year, thus it was a tremendous excitement for them all to see a strange ship and its still stranger occupants. The women crowded on board delighted with our gramophone, amazed at our clothes, simply enraptured with the zip fasteners some of us had on our jackets. The women were all dressed up for the occasion, and very beautiful some of them looked. They wore bright red seal-skin boots ornamented with a mosaic of different-coloured pieces of seal skin, seal-fur trousers, a close-fitting blouse of some bright-coloured material, and above that a most exquisite short cape of minute beads of many different colours, worked together into a complicated pattern'.

A number of the excited Cambridge graduates later piled ashore, found a soft piece of turf on which to party and wound up the gramophone: 'The girls danced a furious double time to it, which was most exhausting'.

ELLESMERE ISLAND, 2007
JOÃO RODRIGUES 1965-

Dr João Rodrigues is a Research Associate based at the Department of Applied Mathematics and Theoretical Physics, University of Cambridge. In 2002 he swapped the warmth of his home country for sub-zero temperatures, tailoring 20 years of work in theoretical physics in Lisbon to the study of Arctic sea ice. He is currently building the scientific team to make best use of ice thickness data obtained by the adventurer Pen Hadow on his 2009 Arctic Ocean expedition.

Rodrigues was photographed outside Eureka Weather Station, Ellesmere Island, on 31 October 2007. He had just arrived back from several hours drilling bore holes in the sea ice in the dark, calibrating an ice-penetrating radar, in temperatures hovering around −40°C. When asked about this portrait, over email at home back in Cambridge, Rodrigues was typically modest: 'I can't possibly think of a single reason to be in the company of all those distinguished polar explorers and scientists, but that's up to you. I'm no good at captions, I'm going to go for a G&T to get some inspiration. Failing that, I'll ask Sarah, my wife. She should know something good to say'.

SCOTT BASE, 1958
SIR VIVIAN FUCHS 1908-1999

Well-fed, exhausted but happy, Vivian Fuchs is about to take a bath – the first for over three months – having just completed an epic 2,000-mile crossing of Antarctica. This unique portrait was taken on 2 March 1958, shortly after his arrival at the New Zealand Scott Base. Later, whilst in the bath, Fuchs received a congratulatory telegram from Queen Elizabeth, the expedition's patron, informing him of his knighthood.

A polar veteran, known to his friends as 'Bunny', Fuchs was a charismatic leader and diplomat, Director of the British Antarctic Survey and later President of the Royal Geographical Society. He read Natural Sciences at St John's College, Cambridge, where his tutor was Sir James Wordie, the geologist and senior scientist on Shackleton's *Endurance* expedition. Wordie took Fuchs on an expedition to Greenland in 1929, an experience that was to prove a major influence on his life. Fuchs later completed a PhD on the geology of the Rift Valley and made a number of expeditions to central Africa. At the end of an expedition in 1934, accompanied by his wife Joyce, Fuchs drove home overland in their 1929 box-bodied Chevrolet, covering over 8,000 miles in forty-six days. This was just a prelude to the pioneering journey that would become the defining achievement of his long polar career.

George Lowe was the official photographer on Fuchs' triumphant Commonwealth Trans-Antarctic Expedition, a journey described as 'the last great exploration on earth left to man'. Lowe's photography was remarkable and prolific, shooting for almost eighteen months with two Rolleiflex cameras in 'black-and-white for newspapers and advertising'. He also used a Leica for colour transparencies 'for lectures and journals'. At Shackleton Base, Lowe had a prefabricated dark room, beautifully equipped by Kodak. Photography was both recreation and morale booster. 'In fact', he later wrote, 'one of our chief entertainments was taking pictures of each other. We devoted one complete wall of the hut to a Rogue's Gallery, and every week or ten days I tried to get together a new series to put up there. These were our only pin ups!'

During the crossing itself, Lowe kept his equipment in a 'hot box' he had devised, lined with insulation and securely stowed away in the back of Sno-Cat *Haywire*. From the South Pole he flew a batch of film back to London, and developed the remainder at Scott Base using a stainless steel tank with a primus stove burning underneath it. He kept his developing solutions in his Thermos flask. Lowe was typically modest, 'manipulating three cold cameras with two hands can be very frustrating'.

SCOTTISH HIGHLANDS, 2006

SIR WALLY HERBERT 1934-2007

Sir Wally Herbert died in June 2007, Britain's preeminent polar traveller, and the last of the great pioneers. His achievements brought him limited fame during his lifetime and his impact on the landscape of exploration is still to be fully appreciated. Not only a man implausibly tough and experienced, in a rare combination of abilities he was also a beautiful writer and a gifted artist. Few explorers have ever had such an array of talents.

Herbert made history in 1968-69, when he led an expedition with dog-sleds from Point Barrow, Alaska, to the North Pole, via the Pole of Inaccessibility, to become the first man without doubt to have reached the Pole on foot. Along with his three companions and their 40 dogs, he then continued across the ice to reach Spitsbergen, thereby completing the first traverse of the Arctic Ocean. The scientific programme, conducted during the 3,620-mile, 16-month-long trek by Dr Roy 'Fritz' Koerner, was the first surface survey of the frozen polar ocean. Koerner's findings now provide benchmark data for today's scientific predictions about the status of the melting polar ice cap and associated climate change issues. Though this formidable achievement was overshadowed by the Apollo moon-landing, it stands today as one of the greatest expeditionary journeys of all time.

During the course of 40 years Herbert travelled over 23,000 miles through the polar regions and mapped large swathes of unknown Antarctic territory. He later lived among the Greenland Inuit of the High Arctic with his wife and young daughter. His numerous books contributed greatly to people's knowledge of the native Inuit of northwest Greenland. In recognition of his contribution to the understanding of the polar world, a mountain range and plateau were named after him in the Antarctic, as well as the most northerly mountain in Svalbard.

This intimate portrait was secured at his tiny crofter's cottage in the Scottish Highlands, shortly before Herbert passed away. In his final years he continued to enjoy writing, painting and offering advice and support to many later adventurers, most wishing to emulate his achievements on the ice. He was finally awarded a knighthood in 2000 in the Millennium Honours list. Herbert was, according to Sir Ranulph Fiennes, 'the greatest polar explorer of our time' and a man whose determination and courage, according to The Prince of Wales, were 'of truly heroic proportions'. Others have a more intimate view of the explorer: 'Wally was a gentle and much loved person, ever so humble, yet so very brave and brilliant'.

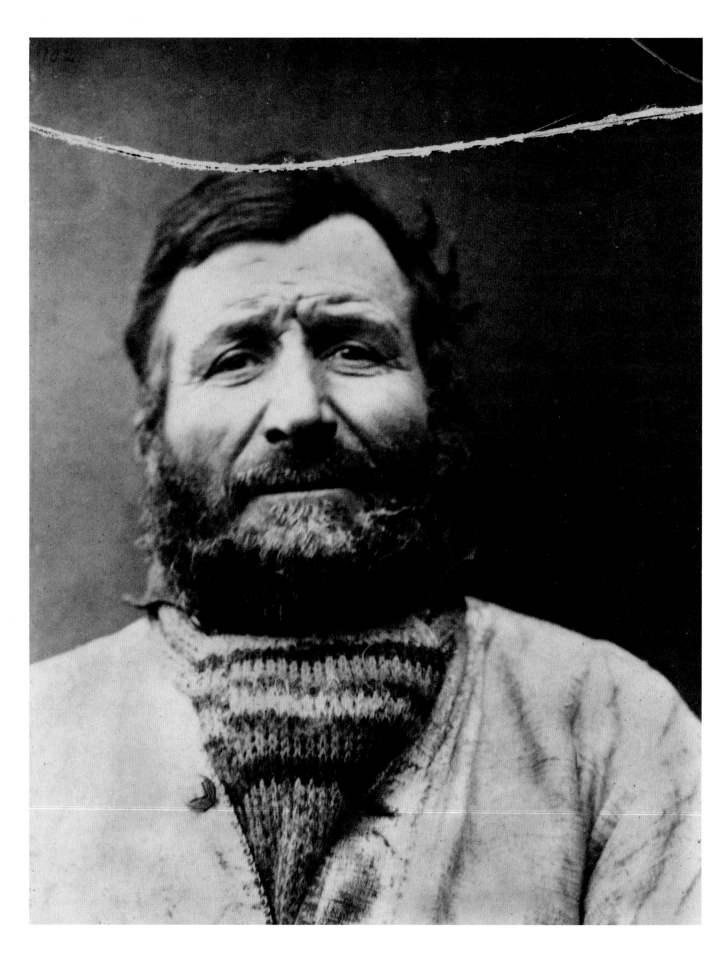

SHETLAND ISLANDS, 1888
PETER SINCLAIR 1840-n.d.

This is one of 113 photographs in a rare album in the collections of the Scott Polar Research Institute, taken during the whaling voyages of *Eclipse* in the Greenland Sea in 1888 and of *Maud* to Davis Strait and Baffin Bay the following year. The photographer was Walter Livingstone-Learmonth, rancher and big-game hunter, who joined the whaling voyage in order to shoot polar game. The *Eclipse* was captained by David Gray, renowned whaler from Peterhead, the most easterly town in Scotland and for long the principal whaling port in the world. In a whaling career that spanned five decades, Captain Gray made 49 voyages to the Arctic seas.

Launched in Aberdeen in 1867, the *Eclipse* was built specially for Gray's command. She cost almost £12,000 and carried eight whaleboats and a crew of 55 men. The Shetland-born Peter Sinclair was a seaman and later ice-master on a number of whaling voyages. He joined *Eclipse* at Lerwick as she made her way north, sails set for the Greenland Sea. Sir Arthur Conan Doyle was sufficiently impressed by the hardy Shetland whalers, many of them veterans from the Royal Navy and weathered by long careers amongst the ice, that he included a portrait of Sinclair in an article about the fishery, entitled 'The Glamour of the Arctic'. After her famous career at Peterhead, the *Eclipse* was sold to Dundee in 1893 and later to Norway. Renamed *Lomonosov*, the old ship ended her ocean going days as a research vessel under the Russian flag, registered at Archangel.

LONDON, 2008
MONICA KRISTENSEN SOLÅS 1950-

Dr. Monica Kristensen Solås is one of the world's leading glaciologists and the only living woman recipient of the Gold (Founder's) Medal of the Royal Geographical Society, awarded in 1989 for her 'outstanding contribution to scientific discovery in the Antarctic'. The last woman honoured with that Gold Medal was Dame Freya Stark, in 1942. Kristensen was photographed on a recent visit to London, shortly before giving interviews to the press.

Admitting – with a twinkle in her eyes – that she is 'totally uncompetitive', Kristensen says that she isn't looking for glory or adventure in the Antarctic. She apologises if that sounds slightly boring, for it is the scientific challenge that remains her major impulse, as it was at the very beginning of her polar career. After studying mathematics and physics at universities in Norway, she developed her field-skills while over-wintering for two years on Svalbard, conducting research into the Aurora Borealis. She received a PhD for her work on Antarctic tabular icebergs from the Scott Polar Research Institute in 1983.

In 1986-87, she was leader of an expedition to follow Roald Amundsen's route to the South Pole. After crossing the Ross Ice Shelf, they followed his original route up the Axel Heiberg Glacier, arriving after 39 days of sledging at 86 degrees South. Sacrificing speed for their scientific research, they arrived at this point, some 400km from the Pole, behind schedule. Kristensen then made the most difficult polar decision of all – the decision to turn around – in order to ensure no loss of life to the team of dogs, or her companions. A veteran of many polar expeditions, she continues to lead scientific research on Foxfonna, Svalbard, where dogs rather than snowmobiles remain her chosen mode of field transport.

Celebrated in her native Norway as the 'Snow Queen', Kristensen defies most of the stereotypes of the frostbitten polar tough guy. Yet her charm belies incredible core strength, beyond that of most modern polar travellers, who enjoy brief dalliances with the icy world. 'Antarctica is such a huge, vast place ... the environment certainly affects people's psychology and I don't think you could imagine anything more desolate or frightening'. Kristensen is no stranger to fear, which her male colleagues either encounter less often or admit to less willingly. 'The worst kind of fear is not one you experience immediately. Yes, I have fallen down crevasses a few times – not very deep ones, but ones where I am hanging from the edge by my arms, but everything happens too quickly. There have been other times when we've been in danger for long periods. It's like having danger walking there with you. You don't feel panic, almost nothing at all. It's just this frightening feeling staying with you, eating away at you and that is a strain'.

LONDON, 1910
EDWARD WILSON 1872-1912

Dr Edward Adrian Wilson was assistant surgeon on the *Discovery* expedition, and his remarkable drawings and paintings of the Antarctic landscape are without equal. A deeply religious man, his sympathetic character and genuine care for his shipmates made him one of the most admired on the voyage. Scott relied heavily on Wilson for guidance and moral support.

He has been photographed here, in his favourite tweed suit, sitting in the studio of his friend, the artist Alfred Soord, whilst having his portrait painted. There is something remarkable about seeing the artist at ease, becoming the subject of someone else's painting. Soord's oil canvas was exhibited at the Royal Academy in 1910.

Wilson joined *Terra Nova* as Chief of the Scientific Staff and zoologist, as well as being the expeditionary artist. His kind and selfless nature earned him the affectionate nick-name 'Uncle Bill'. Wilson was an automatic choice as a member of the final South Pole party and he died alongside Scott on the return journey in 1912. At the last, Scott wrote of him: 'He died, as he lived, a brave, true man – the best of comrades and staunchest of friends'. In the years that followed, a great number of Wilson's watercolours and sketches were given to the newly-established Scott Polar Research Institute, where they form a suitable tribute to his artistic legacy.

PATRIOT HILLS, 2003
MARTIN RHODES 1961-

Dr Martin Rhodes, 'Doc Martin' to his many friends, is an expedition and mountain rescue doctor with over 20 years of experience in polar environments. He works with ALE (Antarctic Logistics and Expeditions) and Poles Apart, a specialist consultancy. Rhodes is trained in Accident and Emergency, General Practice, Advanced Trauma Life Support and is also an Advanced Life Support Instructor. He has climbed, trekked and skied extensively throughout the Andes and the Himalaya and has been medical officer to the Everest Marathon.

This portrait was taken inside the medical tent at Patriot Hills, Antarctica. Shortly after this photograph was taken, Rhodes rescued and stabilized Jennifer Murray and Colin Bodill after their near fatal helicopter crash. They were attempting to become the first to pilot a helicopter around the world, from Pole to Pole. They both made full recoveries and completed their circumnavigation in 2007.

Hartley considers Rhodes 'one of the nicest blokes' he has ever met. No surprise, as he has been on the receiving end of his medical skills on more than one occasion. In 2006, he saved three of Hartley's toes when he got severe frostbite. Married to a stunt-woman, Rhodes spends the summer season in Antarctica and much of the rest of the year in the French Pyrenees, where he has a home and can climb in the sunshine.

WEDDELL SEA, 1915
TOM CREAN 1876-1938

The big smiling Irishman from Kerry was a colossal figure in an era that produced so many tales of endurance and survival. He was blessed with formidable physical and mental strength – a man who wouldn't buckle, the type of man you put first on the list, 'as near to being indestructible as any human could be'. Tryggve Gran, the hardy young Norwegian skier, who travelled with Scott in 1910-11, remembered Crean as a man who 'wouldn't have cared if he'd got to the Pole and God Almighty was standing there, or the Devil. He called himself the Wild Man from Borneo and he was'.

Hurley took this stunning portrait on 7 February 1915. Orde-Lees, a shipmate on the *Endurance* voyage, also described Crean in his diary: '[A] fine character, one of the most reliable men … he is an Irishman and a giant at that … his staunch loyalty to the expedition is worth a lot'. He excelled himself on Scott's 1911 expedition when he and Lashly, another naval rating, rescued Lieutenant Teddy Evans, dragging him 50 miles to safety on the back of a sledge, before walking a further 40 miles alone to fetch help. For this heroic act, among so many, he was awarded the Albert Medal for bravery.

Crean wasn't just brute force and bulk. He was modest. He was calm and assured. His irrepressible sense of humour, unbounded optimism and mostly tuneless singing made him essential when spirits were low. At all times, he would either be smoking a pipe, or wearing a wide smile on his face. Crean was one of the very few people to serve both Scott and Shackleton and he outlived them both. He retired to his birthplace, Annascaul, on the west coast of Ireland, where he opened a pub, 'The South Pole Inn', still serving a good pint to this day.

IGLOOLIK, 2008
MARY QULITALIK 1950-

In 2001 Mary Qulitalik was chosen to take part in the pioneering film *Atanarjuat*. Based on an Inuit legend, 'Fast Runner' was the first feature film ever to be written, acted and directed entirely in Inuktitut. *Atanarjuat* was a huge commercial success and went on to win several awards at major international film festivals. Mary became a legend within Nunavut.

Hartley's meeting with the polar film star was fortunate. 'I shot this photograph by pure chance, while in Igloolik airport, as my plane was being re-fuelled en route to Resolute Bay. I saw her marvellous face through the window and waited ages for her to come inside the terminal. It wasn't until I got back onto the plane, and showed another passenger her image in the viewer on the back of my digital camera, that I discovered who it was ... the Gracie Fields of Nunavut!'

The director of *Atanarjuat*, Zacharias Kunuk, is the co-founding president of Isuma, Canada's first independent Inuit production company. Isuma's mission is to produce independent community-based media – films, television, and now the Internet – to preserve and enhance Inuit culture and language, to create jobs and economic development in Igloolik and Nunavut and to tell authentic Inuit stories to Inuit and non-Inuit audiences worldwide. It is clear that much has changed in this community since its first contact with Europeans, when Captain William Edward Parry's HMS *Fury* and HMS *Hecla* wintered in the area in 1822.

PARIS, 1910
HSH ALBERT I, SOVEREIGN
PRINCE OF MONACO 1848-1922

Albert Honoré Charles Grimaldi was born in Paris in 1848 and from a very early age showed a strong fascination for the Arctic. As a young man with an adventurous spirit, not to mention impeccable connections, he travelled widely. He joined the Spanish Royal Navy and later bought a magnificent schooner, the *Hirondelle*, in which he embarked on a number of scientific cruises in the Mediterranean, the Atlantic and the North Sea.

Beginning in 1898, he was able to mount four scientific cruises to Svalbard on his yacht, the second *Princesse-Alice*. The first voyage was a successful oceanographical reconnaissance, whilst also adding to the collections of his Musée Océanographique de Monaco, which had just begun construction. In 1899, bows were pointed north once again and more hydrographical data was obtained. A third cruise, in 1906, added significant meteorological observations to the survey work of the ship and a final voyage in the following year completed this remarkable scientific programme. The Prince showed a keen interest in environmental protection, particularly in Svalbard, and also lent his support to a number of polar expeditions. He was a patron of Shackleton's famous *Endurance* voyage, among many others less well known.

In this portrait, taken in 1910 at the Académie des Sciences de Paris, Prince Albert is proudly wearing his uniform as a member of the Institut de France. In 1915, the Prince celebrated the completion of his last cruise, bringing to an end a long campaign of twenty-eight voyages, and leaving a remarkable legacy to oceanography and deep-sea exploration. He had not forgotten the polar dreams of his childhood: 'I felt a genuine happiness to find once again the vigorous melancholy of Arctic scenes, where bodies and souls grow stronger in a magnificent battle, with the pride of their power and in a serenity lost since the first years of youth'.

NORTH POLE, 2006
HSH ALBERT II, SOVEREIGN
PRINCE OF MONACO 1958-

The only son of Prince Rainier III and the celebrated Hollywood actress Grace Kelly, Albert Alexandre Louis Pierre Grimaldi is the current ruler of the Principality of Monaco. A graduate of Amherst College, Massachusetts and an accomplished sportsman, in particular in yachting and skiing, Prince Albert II has been a member of the International Olympic Committee since 1985. He has competed in five Winter Olympics in the bobsleigh.

The great-great-grandson of Prince Albert I – the pioneering oceanographer and patron of exploration – Prince Albert II continues to use his position to draw public attention to the need for environmental protection. This portrait was taken on 16 April 2006 at the North Pole. In the modern world of polar firsts, Prince Albert has his own record – the first incumbent head of state to have reached the North Pole.

In June 2006, he created the Prince Albert II of Monaco Foundation, dedicated to environmental protection and financing sustainable development. 'The challenge of protecting our environment and implementing measures to enable natural resources to be protected, extends far beyond the borders of each country', Prince Albert II explains. 'By definition, this is a common global challenge that requires urgent and concrete action in response to three major environmental issues: climate change, loss of biodiversity and water. This situation compels each one of us to take action if we want to protect the planet for future generations ... the environment belongs to all of us and it is our duty to protect it. Rest assured of my personal and unfailing commitment towards achieving this goal'.

ANGMAGSSALIK, 1931
HENRY GEORGE 'GINO' WATKINS 1907-1932

Whilst a student at Cambridge, Gino's imagination was stirred by Raymond Priestley's lectures on polar travel and he quickly transferred this interest into action. He led a Cambridge University expedition to Spitsbergen in the summer of 1927 and the following year led an expedition to Labrador to survey the unknown upper reaches of the Hamilton River.

The British Arctic Air Route expedition of 1930-31, which he led, was to be his crowning achievement. Gino was loved by his comrades, with whom he generously shared the credit for their joint successes, and was well respected by polar experts many years his senior. Admiral William Goodenough, President of the Royal Geographical Society, described Gino: 'Slight in figure, quiet, almost soft in voice, there was no prominent feature that called for striking recognition ... men who looked for some mark in face or speech which would display the commanding personality, which after his first two expeditions they knew existed, were almost startled by his youthful appearance'.

This rare photograph was taken in July 1931, probably on the shores of Sermilik Sound. Gino was learning the art of kayaking for a summer journey, by motorboat, down the east coast to the southern tip of Greenland. Whilst surveying at Umivik, Watkins spent most of his time hunting by kayak.

On hearing of Gino's tragic death – he was lost in his kayak off Greenland during a second expedition in 1932 – the polar veteran Hugh Robert Mill, overcome with sadness, immediately wrote a tribute in *The Times*. 'He was little more than a boy in years; altogether a boy in his spirit of optimism, though with all a man's power of steadfast will and with that inborn instinct of leadership which is the rarest and most valuable gift for an explorer. I have known all the Polar explorers of the last half-century, but no one can stand beside young Watkins, save the young Fridtjof Nansen as I met him on his return from the first crossing of Greenland 44 years ago. Both had the charm of a winning personality; both had the clearness of vision to plan great and new ventures and the firmness of mind to carry them through despite all the buffering of fate'.

SEVERNAYA ZEMLYA, 2006
GEORGES BAUMANN 1967-

In 2006, Georges Baumann attempted to do a land-to-land crossing of the Arctic Ocean, from Russia to Canada via the North Pole. That year there were five expeditions leaving from Severnaya Zemlya, of which three teams eventually chose to get air-lifted over the dangerous thin ice near the coast. Baumann and another adventurer, Thomas Ulrich, decided to make 'pure' attempts and go straight from land.

Before leaving, however, after one night camping out on his own, Baumann wasn't confident about the thickness of the ice. He made a satellite call to his five-year old son, who said: 'Daddy if you love me so much why have you gone so far away?' At that point he decided not to go, but to face his sponsors and wait for another year and better conditions. His was one of the bravest decisions that year. In contrast, Ulrich set off across the ice and after two days phoned for help, calling for urgent emergency rescue.

Born in Berne in 1967, Baumann spent most of his childhood in the ski resort of Gstaad. The Swiss Junior Karate champion, he is now a personal bodyguard. Most of his time is spent in the mountains, or on the shores of Lake Geneva where he lives with his family. He is now planning to repeat an attempt to cross the Arctic Ocean to raise awareness and money for two charities: Innocence in Danger, the international child protection movement to combat paedo-criminality and ELA, an association that supports patient care and research into the leukodystrophies, a group of rare genetic disorders that affect the central nervous system. Whilst some critics question the value of recent polar 'exploration' – where adventurers explore little, instead race for new records – when these trips realise their potential in raising money for charitable causes then the value of modern expeditions is easy to see.

WEDDELL SEA, 1915
SIR JAMES WORDIE 1889-1962

James 'Jock' Wordie, the geologist on Shackleton's *Endurance*, was a very popular member of the expedition, dryly humorous and engagingly clever. He had set his heart on going south whilst at Cambridge. He had attended a dinner there with Lady Scott, Captain Scott's widow, and she had tried 'to dissuade all would-be candidates from the thought of going with Shackleton'.

In 1914, he joined the Imperial Trans-Antarctic Expedition as chief of the scientific staff and endured all of the perils of a voyage that would become famous. In spite of its failure and the considerable rigours of being beset then abandoned on the ice, he brought back important geological specimens and useful oceanographic observations.

Wordie returned in 1917 to a country at war, joined the Royal Artillery, and saw active service in France. On his demobilization he returned to the polar regions – twice on voyages to Spitsbergen, and later during a long series of expeditions to Greenland and the Canadian Arctic. He became a Fellow of St John's College, Cambridge, eventually rising to become its Master. He was a founder member of the Scott Polar Research Institute and from 1951 the President of the Royal Geographical Society. In later years, he was the elder statesman of polar exploration, encouraging young explorers and scientists in their endeavours.

KILCHOAN, 2008
TREVOR POTTS 1950-

Trevor Potts is best known for being the leader of the only unsupported expedition to successfully repeat Sir Ernest Shackleton's legendary escape from Antarctica. In 1993, Potts and his team built a replica of the 22-foot *James Caird*, the redoubtable whaleboat that survived crossing 800 nautical miles of the Southern Ocean; the most feared piece of water on the planet. Even today, large ships are swamped and sunk by the enormous waves that are generated in the inhospitable seas around Antarctica. Potts survived four gales during the journey, including a severe storm force 10 on their final approach to the island, to arrive on 5 January 1994, the anniversary of Shackleton's death.

The struggle from Elephant Island to South Georgia is only a small part of the *Endurance* epic. After 17 days at sea, Shackleton's team finally landed on the uninhabited south coast of the island, then unmapped, and had to cross treacherous mountains and glaciers on foot to reach the safety of a whaling station on the other side of the island. More than a year after the *Endurance* was crushed, and over three months since he set sail on his rescue mission, Shackleton returned to Elephant Island to save the rest of his men. Not a single member of the party was lost. In 2001, Potts returned to South Georgia to follow Shackleton's footsteps across the island from King Haakon Bay to Stromness. In doing so, he became the only person to have successfully repeated Shackleton's odyssey unsupported.

In addition to his Antarctic exploits, in 1989, Potts and three other Britons completed a kayak crossing of the Bering Strait from Alaska to Siberia. In 1999, he attempted the first kayak circumnavigation of Bylot Island on the northern end of Baffin Island. A former Director of the British Marine Industry Federation, Potts now divides his time between the shores of the Scottish coasts of Kilchoan, where this photo was taken, and Antarctica, lecturing and sharing his passion for the polar regions aboard cruise ships. He is currently establishing a Field Study centre on his campsite at Ardnamurchan, the most westerly point of the British mainland. He leads guided nature walks from his converted croft house, whilst also finding time to tend to his bees.

WEDDELL SEA, 1956
KEITH DEDMAN 1925-1992

Keith Harold Dedman joined the Air Training Corps in 1942 and completed his training as Flight Observer at the Royal Naval Fleet Air Arm station Piarco in Trinidad shortly before the end of the Second World War. After completing his studies at Jesus College, Cambridge, various peacetime tours as a young officer in the Royal Navy took Dedman to New York, Australia and to waters off northern Norway in HMS *Eagle*, serving under Captain Peter Hill-Norton, later Admiral of the Fleet and Chief of the Defence Staff. In 1955, Dedman completed Special Forces survival training with the Air Intelligence Service Squadron in Bad Tölz, Germany and was soon posted to HMS *Protector* in Port Stanley, Falkland Islands.

The advent of the International Geophysical Year and the further expansion of the Falkland Islands Dependencies Survey (FIDS) stations gave added impetus to hydrographic survey work in Antarctica. Dedman stands on the flight deck, in his immersion suit, before one his many sorties in the ship's hardy Westland Whirlwind helicopter. The 1955-56 tour was memorable for the fact that HMS *Protector* rescued passengers and crew of the icebound MV *Theron*, including Edmund Hillary and Vivian Fuchs, guiding them to safety.

A favourite in the officer's mess, Dedman was equally at home with his crews on the playing field, at diplomatic cocktail parties, or singing rugby songs around the piano. After serving in the Antarctic, Dedman was Commander of HMS *Nelson* in Portsmouth, before leaving the Navy for a well-earned retirement. HMS *Protector* served as Royal Navy Guard Ship maintaining British presence in Antarctica and the southern oceans for fourteen seasons up to 1968, when she was replaced by HMS *Endurance*.

IQALUIT, 2007
WILL STEGER 1943-

The American adventurer Will Steger has become a prominent spokesperson for the understanding and preservation of the polar world. Born in 1943 in Richfield, Minnesota, Steger studied as a geologist and was for a number of years a secondary-level science teacher. In 1970 he moved to Ely, where he founded a winter school and developed innovative courses for adapting to life in the wild. A pioneer of adventure-based outdoor education, Steger took to the polar regions to spread his message to a global audience. This photograph was taken at the start of his most recent expedition, Global Warming 101. Steger is looking at the changing weather, the day before beginning his journey across Baffin Island.

In 1986, he completed a dogsled journey to the North Pole without re-supply and during 1988, a 1,600-mile south-north traverse of Greenland – then the longest unsupported dogsled expedition in history. The following year, he embarked upon a 3,471-mile traverse of Antarctica. Steger's record-breaking career continued in 1995 with his International Arctic Project – the first dogsled traverse of the Arctic Ocean from Russia to Canada's Ellesmere Island. For these feats he has been bestowed with honours. In 1995, he was awarded the National Geographic Society's John Oliver La Gorce Medal for 'accomplishments in geographic exploration, in the sciences, and for public service to advance international understanding' and in 2007 he received the coveted Lowell Thomas Award from the Explorers Club for his ongoing work on raising awareness of global warming.

Steger founded the Global Center of Environmental Education at Hamline University in 1991 and the World School for Adventure Learning at the University of St. Thomas in 1993. In 2006, he launched the Will Steger Foundation dedicated to creating programmes that foster international leadership through education. His innovative expedition dispatches over the Internet have ensured him a huge audience. For Steger, a career of polar travel has now become an inspirational means to encourage action, to empower and to enliven the environmental conscience.

For the Scott Polar Research Institute from V. Stefansson *There I am myself in Arctic garb* January 29 [...]

NEW HAMPSHIRE, 1957
VILHJALMUR STEFANSSON 1879-1962

Vilhjalmur Stefansson, 'Stef' to his close companions, was born in a log cabin in Arnes, Manitoba, the son of Icelandic immigrants. Abandoning his theological studies at Harvard Divinity School, Stefansson joined the Anglo-American Polar Expedition, travelling to the Arctic in 1906. Over the course of a prodigious career he made further expeditions into the Alaskan and Canadian Arctic and published some 24 books on his travels and anthropological observations.

Despite considerable successes, controversy surrounds Stefansson's reputation. His attempts to raise reindeer on Baffin Island failed and his effort to create a colony on Wrangel Island in 1923 ended with the death of several members of the party. Stefansson came to realise the wealth of natural resources in the Arctic and actively promoted the economic development of the region. Anthropologists and ethnographers still debate the value of his work. Though conflicts over leadership positions on his expeditions are also well documented, a balanced appraisal of Stefansson's achievement reveals his immense contribution to the knowledge of the polar world.

In 1941 Stefansson married Evelyn Baird and they moved from New York to Vermont, before settling in Hanover, New Hampshire, where he continued his long career of research and public diplomacy as Director of Polar Studies at Dartmouth College; now the permanent home of his 25,000 volume library. Stefansson presented this unusual portrait – one of his favourites – in 1958. He scribbled in blue ink across his white parka: 'To the Scott Polar Research Institute, from one of its Admirers ... [Here I am not in Arctic garb]'. Devoted to good research, not to mention accurate planning, a more familiar Stefansson saying was: 'Adventure is a sign of incompetence'.

LONDON, 2008
STEPHEN JONES 1966-

Jones is the Field Operations Manager in charge of the international base Patriot Hills in Antarctica operated by Antarctic Logistics and Expeditions. As a polar guide, he has led groups to both North and South Geographic Poles and on expeditions to Alaska, Arctic Canada, Greenland and Spitsbergen. He has helped several polar adventurers including Pen Hadow, Hannah McKeand and Rosie Stancer to organise their solo polar expeditions and acts as a consultant to extreme adventures all over the world. He works as a consultant in safety management and crisis management, based on his personal experiences of treating casualties, a terrorist bombing in London and coordinating a three-day rescue of five stranded climbers on the Vinson Massif in Antarctica in 2006.

This portrait was taken in the back garden of Martin Hartley's house in London, with Jones wearing Inuit-style snow goggles. The Inuit invented the world's first sunglasses by carving slits in bone or antler to protect their eyes from the glare of the sun at northern latitudes.

Jones has wide-ranging expedition experience and has planned and managed over 80 conservation, community and adventure projects for Raleigh International with project partners ranging from CARE International and Save The Children, to National Park Authorities and the Natural History Museums in London and Santiago. As a climber, he enjoys remote expeditionary mountaineering and has climbed in Antarctica, the Russian Caucasus in winter, reached the summit of Denali three times and made twelve first ascents in Greenland.

NEW YORK, 1910
MATTHEW HENSON 1866-1955

Matthew Henson was only twelve when he walked from his home in Washington to Baltimore, Maryland, in search of a job. He signed on as a cabin boy on the three-masted merchant ship *Katie Hines*. Under the tutelage of Captain Childs, Henson became a skilled able seaman. After Childs' death, and suffering from the prejudice he experienced from white sailors, he left his life at sea. Henson eventually found another job as a clerk at a clothing store in Washington.

It was here that he would meet the young Robert Peary, then an officer in the US Navy Corps of Civil Engineers, who had come into the shop to buy a pith helmet, before leaving for his next surveying assignment to the jungles of Nicaragua. Peary offered Henson a job as his personal assistant on the trip, where his skills as a mechanic, navigator and carpenter were of great use. Two years later, in 1891, Peary had been granted leave from the Navy to do more exploration in Greenland and he invited Henson to join him.

In Henson, Peary had found an experienced, gifted companion willing to travel to the ends of the earth to support his polar obsessions. In Peary, Henson found a well-disposed sponsor who valued his talents, without whom he had little hope of satisfying his own thirst for adventure. Henson's sledging skills and his command of Inuit languages were to prove invaluable to Peary. Henson was to spend the next eighteen years with Peary on Arctic explorations, most famously participating in their North Pole expedition in 1908-09.

Yet, the renown that Peary courted brought little reward for Henson, who spent the next thirty years working as a clerk in the New York Customs House. He was three times refused a pension by Congress. It wasn't until 1937, at the age of 70, that Henson belatedly achieved some recognition. He was made an honorary member of the Explorers Club and later was awarded a gold medal from the Chicago Geographic Society. Henson died in 1955 and was buried in a small plot at the Woodland Cemetery in the Bronx.

In 1987, after lobbyists decried the neglect of his memory, the remains of Henson and his wife were re-interred in Arlington National Cemetery, a more fitting location for a genuine American hero. Long overdue, in 2000 the National Geographic Society posthumously awarded Henson its highest honour – the Hubbard Medal – accepted on his behalf by his great niece. His memorial in Arlington bears an inscription from his autobiography: 'The lure of the Arctic is tugging at my heart. To me the trail is calling. The old trail. The trail that is always new'.

GJOA HAVEN, 2003
INUIT WOMAN 1948-

On 1 April each year Gjoa Haven celebrates Hamlet Day. The King William Island Netsilik community gets together for activities including snow sculpture and igloo-building competitions, singing, feasts and a parade. Dressed in her traditional parka, this local woman has just led her grandchildren in the treasure hunt. Without a word, she runs away moments later, jumping on the back of a snowmobile.

'This lovely Inuit lady was actually the winner of the ski-doo race', Hartley describes. 'All the elders of the community sped around the bay area on their snowmobiles, pulling a sealskin behind them, upon which was balanced an empty gallon petrol container. The skill was to complete the course without the petrol can coming off – not easy to do, at all, but she was a master!' In the past, gatherings like this involved dancing, story-telling and hunting competitions. The Inuktitut name for Gjoa Haven is Uqsuqtuuq, meaning 'lots of fat', such was the abundance of blubbery sea mammals in nearby waters.

WEDDELL SEA, 1915

FRANK WILD 1873-1939

Known to all as 'Frank', John Robert Francis Wild was born in Yorkshire and spent eleven years in the merchant service before transferring to the Royal Navy in 1900. In 1901 he was chosen from over 3,000 applicants to join *Discovery*, on Scott's first expedition to the Antarctic. He was a member of one of the sledge parties to the high plateau. When one of the party was lost over an ice-cliff in a blizzard, Wild kept his head, leading the group back to safety.

A loyal second-in-command on Shackleton's *Endurance* voyage, Wild was hugely respected by his shipmates. According to one, he was 'always calm, cool or collected, in open lanes or in tight corners he was just the same; but when he did tell a man to jump, that man jumped pretty quickly'. Hurley took this portrait on 7 February 1915, the ship having become beset in heavy pack ice.

Wild remained in command of the men on Elephant Island while they awaited rescue. Serving on five expeditions – four with Shackleton – Wild was the only man to have spent more of his life in the Antarctic than the colossal Tom Crean. After a hard career as an explorer, Wild reluctantly settled in South Africa as a farmer, and lived his last years in relative penury in Klerksdorp, where he was employed as a storeman at the Bobrasco Mine. Often overlooked, Wild may be regarded as one of the most significant figures in Antarctic exploration.

BAFFIN ISLAND, 2007

PAUL DEEGAN 1970 -

'The polar regions are a horizontal Everest'. This thought struck Paul Deegan whilst skiing across the expanse of a frozen Lake Inari in Finland, a year after reaching the summit of the world's highest mountain. In addition to four expeditions to Everest, Deegan has climbed and trekked in the Andes, Alaska and East Africa. He led an expedition to scale previously unclimbed peaks in the Pamirs of Central Asia and walked along a frozen river in a gorge deeper than the Grand Canyon to reach the ancient Himalayan kingdom of Zanskar.

Deegan's first journey to the Arctic was scuppered when his appendix ruptured one day before departure. But every cloud has a silver lining: two months later a chance opportunity took him to northern Norway with Martin Hartley. Deegan's baggage was mislaid by the airline, causing them to arrive after midnight at a banquet laid on by their Sámi hosts. They were greeted by the first aurora of the year, a steaming plate of roasted reindeer meat and kitchen-sink-sized bowls of fresh cream and wild berries. It was the perfect introduction to the Arctic.

In 2001, he travelled with Glenn Shaw, who has brittle bone disease, to the Antarctic Peninsula to record his successful attempt to kayak off the coast of the continent. In 2007, Deegan joined Martin Hartley to guide a group of novices across Baffin Island with expedition leader Mark Davey: a trip that raised over £150,000 for the Mitchemp Trust children's charity. Deegan currently divides his time between the United States and Britain. He speaks regularly to audiences about his expeditions and adventures and his first book received an award from the U.S. National Outdoor Book Awards. He never wanted to be an 'explorer' but he is happy with the job he has found for himself: 'I wasn't really qualified for anything else, but the trick in life is to travel the world and try to get someone else to help pay for it. It is a dream to earn a living by communicating your passion for places that you have visited'.

SOUTH GEORGIA, 1914
SIR DANIEL GOOCH 1869-1926

Gooch was the grandson of the illustrious railway engineer Sir Daniel Gooch, a technical genius who designed locomotives and who was responsible for laying the first ever Trans-Atlantic telegraph cable. Gooch the younger was educated at Trinity Hall, Cambridge, and in 1897 succeeded his father Sir Henry Gooch as Third Baronet. In 1907 he bought the magnificent Hylands near Chelmsford and spent much time in expanding the estate. Gooch was drafted in as a last-minute substitute dog handler for Shackleton's Imperial Trans-Antarctic Expedition; his qualifications for the job being his considerable wealth, kindness and his skills in following the hunt and breeding greyhounds.

Gooch sailed with the dogs from Liverpool on 26 October 1914, bound for Buenos Aires, where he signed on board *Endurance* as an able seaman. Frank Wild remembered the Knight's contribution: 'There never was a better A.B. afloat than Sir Daniel Gooch. He obeyed orders promptly and was possessed of a keen sense of humour'. Shackleton wrote, 'We all regretted losing his cheery presence when we headed for the South'. This portrait was taken shortly before Gooch, or 'Curly' as he was affectionately known, left the expedition at South Georgia on 3 December 1914. His country home had been requisitioned as a temporary war hospital and he returned to England to help supervise its operation. He funded the medical equipment himself. Over the course of the war the 190-bed hospital treated over 1,500 wounded patients.

RESOLUTE BAY, 2008
BEN SAUNDERS 1977-

Described by *The Times* as 'the next Sir Ranulph Fiennes', Ben Saunders is one of only four in history have skied solo to the North Pole and, at 26, was the youngest to do so by more than ten years. He set out in 2004 with three strangers who agreed to split the costs of logistics. Only Saunders reached the Pole. One was rescued, overcome with frostbite after falling through thin ice, another because of a broken ankle. The third, a Frenchwoman, was never found.

In 2008, Saunders attempted one of the boldest expeditions to the North Pole in recent years, a solo speed record attempt from Ward Hunt Island. Alone and unsupported, this route has only been completed once, by the adventurer Pen Hadow in 2003 in an epic 58-day trek. Ben aimed to reach the Pole in 30 days, and took with him just 30 days of rations. He is photographed here in Resolute Bay, shortly before the start of his attempt. After covering 51 nautical miles in the first week of the expedition, a broken ski binding forced the expedition to a premature end.

Saunders' ambitious SOUTH expedition is due to depart in the autumn of 2008. He hopes to ski to the South Pole and back, covering some 1,800 miles, clocking up one of the longest unsupported polar journeys in history. 'I am not an explorer in the Edwardian sense', Saunders says. 'The maps have been drawn. Everybody knows where the Poles are. I'm exploring human rather than geographical limits'.

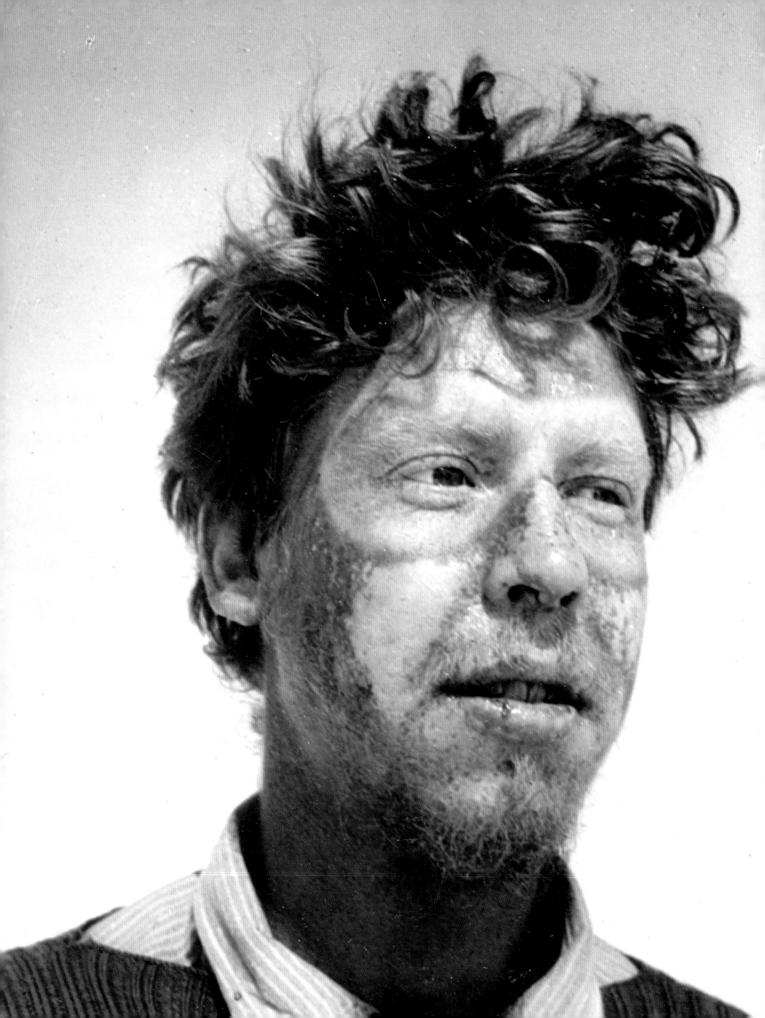

MAUDHEIM, 1951
STIG HALLGREN 1925-n.d.

This is a rare portrait of Stig Hallgren, the young Swedish filmmaker who arrived during the second year of the Norwegian-British-Swedish Antarctic Expedition of 1949-52. It was a hugely successful expedition, one of the first to lead to genuine international cooperation in Antarctica, but it was marred by tragedy. Hallgren survived to tell the harrowing tale. This photograph was taken just moments after his return to safety.

One evening, having just arrived at Maudheim, he went out for a test-drive in the newly repaired Weasel, a powerful tracked vehicle designed for heavy transport on the ice. Three companions, the Swedish mechanic Knalle Ekström, radio operator Leslie Quar and the young Australian physicist John Jelbart, joined him. The vehicle, driven by Ekström, set out for the quay to pick up a supply of seal meat, recently unloaded from the ship *Norsel*. Suddenly a bank of fog rolled in, disorientating the party, and they careered at speed straight over the edge of the ice cliff into the sea. His companions were never seen again.

Hallgren managed to swim to the safety of an ice floe two hundred yards off, but soon realised that it wouldn't hold his weight. He dived back into the freezing water and climbed onto a larger floe, levering himself up by using a sheath knife that was luckily in his back pocket. He spent thirteen hours walking round the ice floe to keep warm, knowing that if he sat down that night he would freeze to death. He drifted out with the tide and was later spotted some miles distant. Once rescued, Hallgren insisted on walking unaided the whole way back to the base. 'The fact that Stig was able to stand the frightful strain, physical as well as mental', wrote his leader some time after the accident, 'was undoubtedly due to his being an exceptionally strong swimmer and powerful athlete in thorough training, who, despite his kindly, gentle ways, is hard as nails'.

SIBERIA, 2004
DOMINICK ARDUIN 1961-2004

On March 5 2004, just moments after this portrait was taken, the French woman Dominick Arduin left for the North Pole on a supported, solo expedition. Five expeditions were leaving from Cape Artichesky that season. A big open water lead just off the starting point posed an immediate problem. Arduin decided to ski and paddle across this 55 km stretch, in pursuit of a 'pure' North Pole journey (which must start from land). She estimated that her crossing to solid ice would take at least 2 days. An avid canoeist living in Lapland, she was used to these harsh conditions.

Arduin had made an attempt to get to the North Pole from Russia in 2003, but it was cut short after she fell through the ice. She was rescued, but most of her toes had to be amputated due to frostbite. For the previous 15 years she had worked as a guide in Finnish Lapland and received dual citizenship. She said that she had grown up in the Alps, had been orphaned at an early age, and that she had recently recovered from cancer. Her life story was one of overcoming adversity and a single-minded pursuit of her dreams. Sadly, her polar ambitions would prove fatal.

Her last words to Martin Hartley after he had taken her photograph were 'I want a real expedition, not that f**king bulls**t', as she gestured toward three other teams who were being airlifted, over the dangerous thin ice, some 36 nautical miles closer to the Pole. The next day, a full moon rose. Several North Pole teams reported issues with their ARGOS positioning beacon. Arduin's beacon transmitted only faint signals. The full moon and an approaching storm both set the Arctic Ocean in motion, breaking up the ice with the pans colliding in a dark, cold torrent. Somewhere, in the midst of it all, was a brave woman who refused to compromise her goals. She was never seen again.

138   POLAR PORTRAITS FACE to FACE

WASHINGTON, 1911
ROBERT PEARY 1856-1920

Born in Cresson, Pennsylvania, Robert Edwin Peary graduated from Bowdoin College, Maine, in 1877. At 23 he found employment as a draughtsman with the US Coast and Geodetic Survey in Washington at a salary of $10 a week. The posting was an improvement on previous occupations – at various times he had been a local surveyor and a jobbing taxidermist – but the ambitious young man was dissatisfied. 'I don't want to live and die without accomplishing anything or without being known beyond a narrow circle of friends', he wrote shortly afterwards. Peary was driven by an insatiable desire to prove himself. Aged 30 he wrote, 'Remember, mother, I must have fame, and I cannot reconcile myself to years of commonplace drudgery and a name late in life when I see an opportunity to gain it now and sip the delicious draught while I yet have youth and strength and capacity to enjoy it to its utmost ... I want my fame now'.

It was to the Arctic that he directed his gaze and to the North Pole in particular. Unlike most previous explorers, Peary studied Inuit techniques of survival and travel and became a master of sledging, albeit that his navigation and cartography were often proved inaccurate and at other times made up altogether. After eight expeditions via Greenland and Ellesmere Island, he reached it in 1909. 'The Pole at last!!!' he wrote. 'The prize of 3 centuries, my dream and ambition for 23 years. Mine at last'. He was awarded a hero's welcome in the United States and thanked, rightly, for his expeditionary endeavours. After some bitter public debate with a rival claimant, Dr Frederick Cook, Congress officially recognised Peary's achievement. He was granted the rank of Rear Admiral in 1911 and appears here proudly in uniform in a rare studio portrait. Peary was buried with full honours at Arlington National Cemetery in 1920. His wife, Josephine Diebitsch Peary is buried with him.

On the thirteenth anniversary of his discovery of the North Pole in 1922, the National Geographic Society unveiled its white granite tribute to the explorer. The monument, with its smooth terrestrial globe, bears the Latin inscription: 'Inveniam Viam Aut Faciam', meaning 'I shall find a way or make one'. These words, Peary's personal motto, well describe his staunch determination to overcome all obstacles to claim the prize. Yet, lingering doubts remain and subsequent analyses have concluded that he probably falsified his readings and came, at best, within 96 kilometres of the Pole. Despite this, given the equipment available at the time, and bearing in mind his other journeys, it is fair to say that Peary's contribution to polar exploration was considerable. His remarkable, pioneering achievements as an explorer go far beyond his controversial 1909 expedition.

ARCTIC OCEAN, 2006
VICTOR BOYARSKY 1961-

Dr Victor Boyarsky was a member of the International Trans-Antarctica dog-sled expedition, 1989-90, a huge 7-month journey of some 6,500km. He was co-leader of the International Arctic Project Expedition in 1995, and since 1997 has guided more than 18 Arctic tourist trips, in which participants simply ski the last degree to the North Pole. He is founding director of the Russian Agency VICAAR, as well being a director of the Russian State Museum of the Arctic and Antarctic in Saint Petersburg. Boyarsky has achieved extraordinary success in guiding and logistics and is now one of the world's most experienced polar travellers. He has been to the North Pole over 50 times.

The day this portrait was taken Boyarsky was very concerned as he stared out the window of the huge Russian Mi-6 helicopter, surveying the state of the sea ice. He was just about to drop off the adventurer Thomas Ulrich near Cape Artichesky, at the beginning of his solo unsupported Trans-Arctic expedition. Two days later Ulrich called Boyarsky on his satellite telephone, shouting 'I'm dying, I'm dying, you have to get me out of here!' A hugely expensive and risky rescue operation was launched to save Ulrich's life, just two days after he had left the coast.

GODHAVN, 1869
INUIT BOY 1860- n.d.

This portrait appears in *The Arctic Regions*, published in London in 1873 to huge fanfare. Queen Victoria headed the list of subscribers. The book's 141 photographs, hand-pasted within the text, were a sensation. Although only 350 copies of this book were printed, its significance lies not only in that it was the first published work to include photographs of the polar regions, but also because of their range and quality. *The Art Journal* claimed that *The Arctic Regions* would 'form the most instructive work on the frozen seas that has ever appeared'.

Chartering the *Panther*, a sealing vessel with auxiliary steam power, the artist William Bradford had set off in the summer of 1869, bound up the Greenland coast as far above the Arctic Circle as ice permitted. Reaching Melville Bay before being forced to turn back by impenetrable pack ice, he returned with scores of oil studies, sketchbook drawings and over 300 photographs.

This portrait was taken by the Bostonian studio photographers Dunmore and Critcherson, as the *Panther* made her way up the west coast of Greenland. Bradford described the scene in his journal: 'Esquimaux wide awake. He kept his eye on the Camera while being photographed, expecting it would go off or hurt him'. Other photographs became a sketchpad for Bradford's grand compositions – he based many of his famous oil paintings on views captured on this voyage. The photographs were also displayed in New York, projected by a lantern upon an enormous screen.

RESOLUTE BAY, 2008
INUIT BOY 2000-

Resolute is a small Inuit hamlet on Cornwallis Island in Nunavut, Canada. It is situated at the northern end of Resolute Bay and is part of the Qikiqtaaluk Region. At 74°41'N, Resolute is one of Canada's northernmost communities, second only to Grise Fiord on Ellesmere Island. It is also one of the coldest inhabited places in the world, with an average yearly temperature of −16 degrees.

Founded in 1947 as the site of an airfield and weather station, it was named after the British exploration vessel HMS *Resolute*. Efforts to assert sovereignty in the Arctic led the Canadian federal government to relocate Inuit there by forced settlement. The first group arrived in 1953 from Inukjuak, Quebec, and Pond Inlet, Nunavut. Having lost most of their traditional skills and purpose, Inuit residents are now to a large degree dependent on government support. There are currently about 250 people living in the settlement. Resolute Bay airport is still the main core of the town, largely serving as an aviation hub for wealthy travellers. Martin Hartley was in town to photograph a polar adventurer training for a new expedition. Though the temperature was −35 degrees – challenging conditions for most visitors – this young local boy wasn't bothered at all, sledging with his mates on a pile of snow outside the grocery store.

On 10 August 2007, Prime Minister Stephen Harper announced the plans for the construction of a pair of year-round multimillion-dollar military facilities within the contested waters of Canada's Arctic territory. The facilities consist of a deep-sea port at Nanisivik and a new army training centre at Resolute. A statement issued by the Prime Minister described the development as 'supporting Arctic training and operations ... to provide an increased capability and faster response time in support of regional military or civilian emergency operations'. Once completed, the naval station will likely be home to a new fleet of ice-breaking patrol ships and Canada's Victoria-class submarines. It is clear that the landscape of the Arctic is changing as never before, both environmentally and geopolitically.

SOUTH ATLANTIC, 1914
LIONEL GREENSTREET 1889-1979

A young officer of the merchant service, temporarily out of work, Greenstreet signed on to the *Endurance* at short notice – just 24 hours before the ship sailed from Plymouth – when the original first officer withdrew to join the war effort. Hard-working and perceptive, and always first to offer a rude joke, he was well-liked by the crew and became a close friend of Frank Hurley, who took his portrait onboard *Endurance* in 1914. Writing to his father, Greenstreet expressed his admiration for his new companion: 'Hurley is a warrior with his camera and would go anywhere or do anything to get a picture'.

After serving on rescue tugs during both the First and the Second World War, Greenstreet retired to Devon, although he still enjoyed riotous dinners at his London Club and at naval reunions. 'He always had a twinkle in his eye, full of fun and playing jokes', his nephew described. 'One always felt that he was up to some sort of mischief. He lived his life to the full'. He was mistakenly reported as dead in 1964 and took great pleasure in informing the newspapers that his obituary was premature. Humorous to the end, he died in March 1979, at the age of eighty-nine, the last of the *Endurance* survivors.

ELLESMERE ISLAND, 2007
MICHAEL GORMAN 1945-

Dr Michael Gorman has developed the innovative technology for Pen Hadow's proposed survey of the Arctic Ocean in 2009. Gorman has invented SPRITE, a robust and portable ice-penetrating impulse radar. He is photographed here at Eureka Weather Station, Ellesmere Island, very happy after a long day of testing his equipment on the ice. SPRITE will be mounted behind Hadow's sledge-boat as he makes his polar crossing. Where possible, raw data (an estimated 5 million readings) will be collected every 20cm along the 2,000km survey route.

The data is processed by an onboard computer, compressed and then uplinked, via the Iridium Satellite network, for the use of scientists back in Britain. It is envisaged that the expedition's website in 2009 will display daily updates on the thickness of the Arctic sea ice and, with further analysis of the data, scientists may be able to predict with greater accuracy the nature and extent of polar warming. Current estimates suggest that within 20 years the Arctic Ocean may be ice-free during summer.

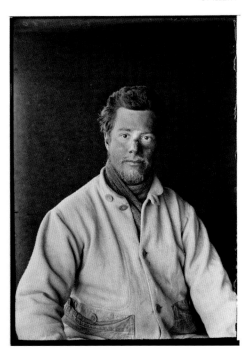

CAPE EVANS, 1912
APSLEY CHERRY-GARRARD 1886-1959

The son of a distinguished Major-General, the young Apsley George Benet Cherry-Garrard – known to all as 'Cherry' – inherited a double fortune in 1907 and shortly afterward embarked on a cruise around the world in cargo boats. When in Brisbane, he heard that Captain Scott was planning a second expedition to the Antarctic and immediately offered his services. With Edward Wilson recommending him, Cherry duly enlisted as 'assistant zoologist'. Despite his youth and inexperience, he won the affection of his comrades and before the close of the expedition he had more sledge journeys to his credit than any other surviving member.

Scott was impressed by his efficiency and enthusiasm as a sledger and tent-mate. Wilson chose Cherry as his companion for the Winter Journey in 1911 to obtain specimen eggs from the emperor penguin rookery at Cape Crozier. This hazardous round trip of 120 miles in darkness, through blinding storms and across deadly crevasses, enduring temperatures in below −70°F, is an exploit without parallel. On their return five weeks later Scott described the journey as 'the hardest that has ever been made'. Cherry later wrote up a narrative of the expedition in *The Worst Journey in the World*, a work of incredible literary merit, in which he described polar exploration as 'the cleanest and most isolated way of having a bad time that has ever been devised'.

Cherry laid stores along the southern route for Scott's Pole team. As the support party returned from the Barrier, Ponting was able to catch on camera their exhaustion and relief at having reached safety. Cherry was perhaps the luckiest to have returned. He was told by Scott that it had been a 'toss up' whether he or Oates should continue. Eight months later, he was a member of the search party which discovered the fate of Scott and his men. At his suggestion, the last line of Tennyson's *Ulysses* ('To strive, to seek, to find and not to yield') was inscribed on the cross atop the cairn of snow built to cover the remains of the polar party.

After the struggle of Antarctica, Cherry commanded a squadron of armoured cars in World War I, wrote a number of fine books and in 1939 married Angela Turner, some thirty years his junior. Afflicted, often bed-ridden, by deep bouts of depression he nevertheless cultivated friendships with distinguished men of letters, such as H.G. Wells and Bernard Shaw and men like Mallory of Everest and Lawrence of Arabia, but the Scott tragedy continued to haunt him for the rest of his life.

ELLESMERE ISLAND, 2006
JEAN-GABRIEL LEYNAUD 1971-

Jean-Gabriel Leynaud is an adventure cameraman, based in Paris. His passion for mountaineering has enabled him to film some of today's leading adventurers and scientists in the wildest places on Earth. He has directed documentaries for Canal+, France2, ARTE and National Geographic, climbing active volcanoes, trekking through deep jungles and travelling with his camera from Everest to the South Pole. Leynaud is photographed at Eureka Airport, Ellesmere Island, just about to fly home. He had just spent 99 days on the ice trying to cross the Arctic Ocean. He was frustrated, but happy to be alive.

Accompanied by his partner, Bettina Aller, Leynaud planned to do a complete Arctic crossing from Russia to Canada, via the North Pole. Having reached the Pole on 3 May, after several airdrops of supplies along the way, deteriorating ice conditions prevented them from reaching the Canadian coast. According to a last reported position, they were on the 86th degree when they called the expedition off. In terrible conditions they were averaging just one mile a day. On 8 June, the pair asked to be evacuated and were picked up by a Twin Otter a few days later. Through the windows of the rescue plane they could see miles of open water, unprecedented at this northerly latitude: stark evidence of the widespread melting of the sea ice in recent seasons. When Leynaud's portrait was taken he was both happy and sad: 'We are lucky to be alive, but the Arctic Ocean is dying'.

LONDON, 1845

GRAHAM GORE n.d.-1847

Graham Gore was First Lieutenant of the *Erebus* on her final Arctic voyage. He entered the Navy as a boy in 1820, fought as a young midshipman at the Battle of Navarino and travelled on the *Beagle* when it sailed in Australian waters. He served as mate in the *Terror* during its Arctic voyage of 1836 and was also present at the storming of forts in the Chinese war. He wears the undress uniform of a Royal Navy Lieutenant, according to regulations of 1843, and a blue cap with a band of gold lace around the crown. In its highly-polished peak one can make out the reflection of the ship's rigging, that sunny afternoon in May 1845.

Like Sir John Franklin, this was his first ever photograph, and it would be the last public image of him. 'The more I see of Gore', Franklin later wrote, 'the more convinced am I that in him I have a treasure and a faithful friend'. Commander James Fitzjames described Gore as a man of 'great stability of character, a very good officer, and the sweetest of tempers ... he plays the flute dreadfully well, draws sometimes very well, sometimes very badly, but is altogether a capital fellow'.

LONDON, 2008
KEN MANTEL 1950-

Mantel is founder of The Narwhal Inuit Art Gallery, which celebrated its twenty-fifth anniversary in 2007, and is currently the only venue in Britain where contemporary Inuit art is on permanent display. He is photographed here surrounded by some of the sculpture and graphic prints in his collections. The aim of NIAEF, the gallery's educational arm, is to raise awareness of the Inuit, their culture and religion, through their art.

Overlooked in his early career by the British Antarctic Survey, for being 'too gregarious', Mantel turned his attentions from geology to culture. In 2001 he established a sculpture park at Bajina Basta, Serbia, on a high farming plateau west of Belgrade and close to the Bosnian border. His proud individualism and his genuine, and overwhelming, passion for Inuit art is profound and he continues to inspire others to champion indigenous art forms. In 2008, the Scott Polar Research Institute won a Collecting Cultures grant from the Heritage Lottery Fund for *Arctic Visions*, an innovative acquisition and outreach project to build and exhibit its Inuit art collections and to further its advocacy in Britain.

ANGMAGSSALIK, 1931
JAMESI TASIUSAK 1901 - n.d.

This is another marvellous unpublished portrait from the British Arctic Air Route Expedition of 1930-31. Though the successful expedition returned home with impressive survey results – over seven major journeys, including a coastal voyage and a crossing of the Greenland Ice Cap – its visual haul remains an equally remarkable achievement. Its long-neglected cinematography and photographic work, much of it now housed in the collections of the Scott Polar Research Institute, offers a unique glimpse of expeditionary life in this period.

After the wreck of one of the surveying aircraft (the Gipsy Moth had been smashed by the ice it was tethered to during a blizzard) the Australian surveyor John Rymill was engaged for the most part in trying to salvage it. With the help of W.E. Hampton, the second pilot and engineer, Rymill worked about ten hours a day for two months during the winter and succeeded in crafting a new aeroplane from the wreckage of the old machine and bits of driftwood and canvas. No sooner had they finished mending one machine, when the second aircraft ruptured its undercarriage landing on the ice and they set to work once more.

After this winter-long effort the indefatigable duo were rewarded with the task of crossing the Ice Cap, a 450-mile journey from their eastern base near Angmagssalik across to the west coast. They rigged up a special sledge with an aeroplane compass mounted on the back. To finally reach Holsteinsborg they would have to travel a further 90 miles by sea, so they decided to take Inuit kayaks with them. Having had no experience at all, they went to a nearby settlement to learn the art. The portrait was taken as 'Jamesi', the Inuit hunter tasked with teaching Rymill the necessary skills, enjoys a well-deserved afternoon snooze in the summer sunshine.

CAMBRIDGE, 2008
JULIAN DOWDESWELL 1957-

Julian Dowdeswell is Professor of Physical Geography and a Fellow of Jesus College, University of Cambridge. He uses airborne, satellite and shipborne geophysical tools to study the nature of glaciers and their response to climate change. As Director of the Scott Polar Research Institute, he has responsibility for its strategic development and oversees its multi-disciplinary research programmes, as well as teaching a new generation of polar scientists. The coming years are very exciting ones for SPRI, as it approaches the centenaries of the Heroic Age Antarctic expeditions, whilst continuing to take a leading role in polar science. The Institute's new Polar Museum is due to open in 2010.

Dowdeswell is shown here in the Institute's library, shortly before hearing the news that he had been awarded the Founder's Medal. This is one of the two most prestigious Gold Medals awarded by the Royal Geographical Society and was presented to him on 2 June 2008 at the Society's headquarters in central London, for his work in the encouragement, development and promotion of glaciology.

The Gold Medal originated as an annual gift of fifty guineas from King William IV. It was awarded for the first time in 1831, for the encouragement and promotion of geographical science and discovery. Today, both medals (Founder's and Patron's) are approved by HM Queen Elizabeth II. Dowdeswell joins a long list of distinguished polar recipients, including John Biscoe, Sir John Ross, Sir George Back, Sir James Clark Ross, John Rae, Elisha Kent Kane, Sir George Nares, Sir Douglas Mawson, Lady Jane Franklin, Adolf Erik Nordenskiöld, Karl Weyprecht, Sir Clements Markham, Vilhjalmur Stefansson, Sir James Wordie, Sir Vivian Fuchs, Charles Swithinbank, Sir Wally Herbert and Sir Ranulph Fiennes.

OSLO, 1974
BRIAN ROBERTS 1912-1978

Dr Brian Birley Roberts, or 'B.B.' to the many who knew him, was a hugely admired scholar and polar diplomat. This enigmatic portrait was taken in May 1974 as Roberts was in Oslo attending a conference, shortly before his retirement. With an encyclopaedic knowledge of polar matters – in particular the Antarctic Treaty, which he helped to develop – Roberts was long-serving head of the Polar Regions Division of the Foreign and Commonwealth Office. Roberts was, in many ways, architect of one of the world's most successful international agreements. A scholar and elder statesman, in 1976 Roberts was awarded the Founder's Medal of the Royal Geographical Society, 'for Polar exploration, and for contributions to Antarctic research and political negotiation'.

Roberts was born in Surrey, the son of a medical man. He fondly recollected the moment he decided to become a polar explorer, reading an Arctic thriller in the *Boys Own Paper* as a ten year old. At school his teachers encouraged his enthusiasm for bird watching and photography; interests he continued as a student at Cambridge University, where he also organised expeditions to Iceland and east Greenland. He was later ornithologist on the British Graham Land Expedition, 1934-37, led by John Rymill. Thus, before his twenty-fifth birthday he had led two summer expeditions to Arctic shores and had taken part in a major Antarctic expedition, the first British foray south since Shackleton's *Endurance*.

In later life, as a Research Associate at the Scott Polar Research Institute, Roberts' influence was particularly profound. He undertook the supervision of the library and the information activities of the Institute. His capacity for work was inexhaustible, the depth of his knowledge was unparalleled, but it was for his sensitivity, good humour, and for the kindness he showed to all those interested in the polar regions that Roberts may be most fondly remembered.

PATRIOT HILLS, 2003
CHA-JOON KOO 1960-

Cha-Joon Koo travelled to Patriot Hills, Antarctica, in 2003 to check on the celebrated adventurer Park Young Seok. Cha-Joon Koo is President and Chief Executive Officer of LG Insurance in South Korea, and his company was sponsoring Park Young Seok's bid to walk to the South Pole from Hercules Inlet. On Cha-Joon Koo's first night in Patriot Hills, the usual storm blew down from the mountains and his tent collapsed with him in it. Terrified that he would die if he left his tent to find shelter, Cha-Joon Koo spent the whole night flattened by the storm until, the following morning, one of the guides resident at the camp went over to peg it out properly.

Park Young Seok is a national hero in South Korea. He is the only man ever to have climbed all the world's fourteen 8,000-metre peaks (climbing six in a single year), the highest summits on each continent, and to have reached both the North and South Pole. In the world of modern 'exploration', this is touted as the 'Grand Slam' of extreme adventuring.

OLRICK BAY, 1901
FREDERICK COOK 1865-1940

The desire to become the first man to reach the North Pole was a passion that was the ruin of Dr Frederick Cook. By 1900 he was an explorer of some fame; he had accompanied Robert Peary to the Arctic and voyaged to Greenland. He had served ably on the 1897 *Belgica* expedition to the Antarctic – the first to winter in the southern ice – during which his care had prevented the entire crew from dying of scurvy. Even the polar hero Roald Amundsen described him as 'a man of unfaltering courage, unfailing hope, endless cheerfulness, and unwearied kindness ... his ingenuity and enterprise were boundless'.

This fascinating portrait, in front of a musk ox fur backdrop, was taken on a Kodak by Clarence Wyckoff and Louis Bement – both tourists paying for their passage – on the ship *Erik*, sent to Greenland to offer relief to Peary and his family in the summer of 1901. Cook was physician and second-in-command of this rescue mission.

However, it all began to go badly wrong. In 1906, Cook led an expedition to climb Mt McKinley, North America's highest mountain, and he declared himself the first man to stand at its summit. Two years later Cook returned from a winter in the Arctic and announced that he had been to the North Pole, showing photographs to prove it. In both cases his claims were discounted. He had not been to either place. His deception is to be much regretted, for he was an explorer of real talent. He remained unrepentant to the last: 'I have been humiliated and seriously hurt. But that doesn't matter any more. I'm getting old, and what does matter to me is that I want you to believe that I told you the truth. I state emphatically that I, Frederick A. Cook, discovered the North Pole'. Though his photographs were fakes, many people still believe that he did.

OSLO, 2008
BØRGE OUSLAND 1962-

Photographed at his home in Oslo, Børge Ousland is a renowned explorer, writer and filmmaker. Something of a national hero in Norway, he is widely admired not only for his exploration achievements but also for the core values he promotes: humility, meticulous planning, self-reliance and a sincere appreciation of the natural world. He is not your typical modern 'explorer', keen to perform upon the stage of fame. The most important rule of success in exploration: 'Preparation, and a little luck', Ousland says, with characteristic modesty.

Humble he may be, but Ousland is also driven by an insatiable, competitive urge and, over a long career on the ice, has become the world's leading polar traveller. After working as a North Sea diver and training in the Norwegian Special Naval Forces, Ousland's first major polar adventure was a crossing of Greenland in 1986. He made the first unsupported trek to the North Pole in 1990, doing it again solo and unsupported in 1994 in just 52 days. In 1997 he completed the first unsupported solo crossing of Antarctica, an epic journey of 2,845km in 64 days, experiencing temperatures as low as −56°C.

In 2001 Ousland made the first solo crossing of the Arctic Ocean, from Siberia to Canada via the North Pole, and immediately promised his wife and son that he would no longer venture alone, the single most dangerous way to travel in the wild. In 2006 he reached the North Pole, again, with fellow epic-traveller Mike Horn, this time becoming the first to dare the trek solely in the 24-hour darkness and intense cold of the polar night.

NEW YORK, 1935
CARL PETERSEN 1897-1941

Carl Oscar Petersen was a veteran of two South Pole expeditions and received two Congressional Medals of Honour for his services. Petersen – 'a tall, blond, owl-faced Norwegian' – emigrated to Chicago and became a sergeant in the Army Air Corps. He had operated radios for a Norwegian whaler and for Amundsen at Spitsbergen. After his death at Portland, Maine, Petersen was buried with full honours in Arlington National Cemetery. On Byrd's first foray to Antarctica, Petersen was radio operator, depot tractor driver, and sometime newspaper editor. Admiral Byrd wrote, in 1931, that Petersen was 'a splendid Norwegian with an adventurous nature, one of the ablest and most valuable members of our expedition to the South Pole'.

Petersen was chief radioman and assistant cinematographer on Richard Byrd's second expedition to the Antarctic in 1933-35. This portrait was taken in New York, shortly after his return, as publicity material for his movie of that expedition, *Little America*. 'When speaking of the Byrd Expeditions there has been an understandable tendency to forget their human components and to think, merely, of a group of hard-working, cold-blooded and precise scientists', remarked *The New York Times* upon the film's release in 1935.

'Such problems as the Saturday night bath, the care of luxuriant beards, finding shelter for cattle, feeding the dogs and cooking seal-fat doughnuts for breakfast have not figured in the headlines and hence have been overlooked. *Little America* helps supply the other half of the picture. With a sharp eye to that quality known as human interest, John L. Herrmann and Carl O. Petersen, Paramount cameramen who accompanied the expedition, have turned out a warm and sensible film document which neither glorifies the polar explorers nor presents them as a group of automatons working in an Antarctic laboratory'.

BRISTOL, 2008

DOUG ALLAN 1951-

One of the world's leading wildlife cameramen, Doug Allan is photographed at his home in Bristol, overlooking the zoo, shortly to go on a well-earned holiday in the Caribbean. Scottish-born, Allan graduated with a degree in maritime biology from Stirling University in 1973 and, deciding that hard science wasn't to be his natural habitat, he quickly escaped into the underwater world. He assisted with Cambridge University expeditions in the Red Sea, and found freshwater pearls in the rivers of Scotland, before heading south as a research diver for the British Antarctic Survey in 1976. Over the next ten years he spent four winters and nine field summers in Antarctica and was awarded the Polar Medal for his work. Stirling University recently awarded him an Honorary Doctorate in recognition 'for his services to polar photography'.

He has returned on countless occasions to both the Antarctic and Arctic with a series of high-profile, award winning films and documentaries for television networks the world over. His work is not confined to the polar regions, of course – his assignments in the Andes and the high Himalaya for *Discovery* are most famous – but the pull of the polar regions is inescapable for someone of Allan's incredible talents. In contributing to *The Blue Planet* and, most recently, *Planet Earth* for the BBC he made over thirty filming trips and picked up Emmy and BAFTA awards for his peerless cinematography. When emailed with news of this exhibition back came this typically modest and matter-of-fact automatic reply: 'Doug is out of the office at the moment, filming at the North Pole, likely not on email. He will be in touch shortly'.

WEDDELL SEA, 1915
HUBERHT HUDSON 1886-1942

The son of a minister, Hudson grew up in a tough East End neighbourhood, left school at the age of fourteen and soon joined the merchant service. He joined Shackleton's *Endurance* as a navigation officer. He was regarded as good-hearted company, although he often behaved oddly. 'One never quite knows', wrote one of his shipmates, 'whether he is on the brink of a mental breakdown or bubbling over with suppressed intellectuality'. He earned himself the nickname 'Buddha' after appearing in a bed sheet with a kettle lid tied to his head at a costume party held aboard the ship, early on in the expedition.

Hurley took this portrait of Hudson – with young emperor penguins destined for the cooking pot – on 12 January 1915, shortly before *Endurance* was beset in the ice. Although often the source of fun, Hudson was highly valued – the best catcher of penguins, he almost single-handedly filled the ship's larder and sustained the crews whilst camped on the Weddell Sea Ice and stranded on Elephant Island. Hudson suffered severe frostbite to his hands, which remained deformed for the rest of his life.

Hudson had a particularly bad time on Elephant Island, confined to the makeshift hut coping as best he could with a nervous breakdown and a festering boil on his backside. He recovered to serve in both World Wars. On 15 June 1942, returning home in a convoy from Gibraltar, HMS *Eaglet* was torpedoed and sank. Hudson went down with the ship.

ARCTIC OCEAN, 2006
BETTINA ALLER 1964-

Bettina Aller is one of the first Scandinavian women to have reached the North Pole by ski. When this photograph was taken she had been on the ice for 99 days. She is on the Arctic Ocean, around 160 miles north of Ward Hunt Island. Danish-born Aller and her French boyfriend, the cameraman Jean Gabriel Leynaud, planned to do a complete Arctic crossing from Russia to Canada, via the North Pole. Having reached the North Pole on 3 May, after several airdrops of supplies along the way, deteriorating ice conditions prevented them from reaching the Canadian coast. According to a last reported position, they were on the 86th degree when they called the expedition off. After 97 days on the ice, on 8 June, the pair asked to be evacuated and were picked up by a Twin Otter a few days later.

In 2004, the pair had reached the North Pole from Siberia in a partial crossing, after being airlifted across an open water section just out from Cape Arktichevsky. In 2001, Aller had to abandon a solo attempt after just a week on the ice. Followed constantly by polar bears, she had to keep her gun unpacked, ready to shoot. Unable to wear proper gloves, Aller developed frostbite in two fingers. The mother of two young children, though she was immensely frustrated not make it across in 2006, you can clearly see the relief on her face to be coming home.

COPENHAGEN, 1917

KNUD RASMUSSEN 1879-1933

A Dane, born and raised in Greenland, familiar with the language and customs of the Inuit, and a student of their traditions and history – Rasmussen was not only one of the great explorers of his generation but also a distinguished ethnographer. Of the Greenland Inuit he would write, '... they understand the art of self-preservation, and in the midst of a merciless fight for existence they have created a culture which compels the greatest admiration'. During his own lifetime Rasmussen would also be widely admired, both by the Inuit with whom he worked and lived, and by an adoring Danish public. This portrait was a publicity shot taken in a Copenhagen studio by the filmmaker Peter Elfelt.

As a young man Rasmussen attended the University of Copenhagen, but failed to graduate. Longing to become a writer he began work as a journalist, travelling to Iceland and later to Swedish Lapland to gather material for literary works. At the age of 23 he served as interpreter on the Danish Literary Greenland Expedition of 1902-04 and later wrote the wonderful book *People of the Polar North* detailing his experiences – a notable work among so many

he would write in a long career. In 1910 he and Peter Freuchen established the most northerly of the Danish settlements at Thule to protect the isolated tribe of 'Arctic Highlanders', natives of the Cape York district, from harmful foreign contact. Thule became the base for his extensive exploratory and scientific work in Greenland – some seven expeditions in all. On his final expedition he contracted pneumonia after an episode of food poisoning and died shortly after his return to Copenhagen.

From 1921-24 he explored some 29,000 miles of Arctic North America, an achievement for which he is perhaps most well-known, becoming the first man to make a northwest passage by dogsled. Yet Rasmussen's legacy owes less to his exploration record, than to his profound contributions to the understanding of indigenous culture. On his pioneering traverse he took with him a range of scientific specialists, whilst he assiduously collected and described Inuit songs, poetry and folklore. He devoted most of his later years to sharing his knowledge and to the publication of a life's work devoted to the people of the North.

LONDON, 2000
REINHOLD MESSNER 1944-

Frequently described as 'the greatest mountaineer of all time', Reinhold Messner is best known for being the first person to climb all fourteen 8,000-metre peaks. In 1978 he became the first, with climbing partner Peter Habeler, to reach the summit of Everest without the use of supplemental oxygen. He repeated the feat from the Tibetan side in 1980, during the monsoon season. This was the first time that the world's highest mountain had been climbed solo. Messner has been photographed at the Royal Geographical Society, upon his arrival to London in 2000.

At the end of the 1980s, Messner turned his considerable attention to the polar regions. 'I didn't know how to handle the North Pole, the South Pole and Greenland. I had to learn everything. Amundsen and Scott had reached the South Pole, but the rest was open. I approached Antarctica exactly like Shackleton planned to do it. I copied him. It was too costly for me to go with dog sleds. So I was forced to do it another way. And so I decided to go without anything'. In 1990, Messner became the first person to cross Antarctica on foot. In doing so, he repeated a basic tenet of his mountaineering career. 'I soon found my own style on very small and cheap expeditions. I looked for good partners. And from that moment onwards I was able to finance my own expeditions. My attitude was, let's see, let's go. If we fail we will learn something. Then we will go back. Since my expeditions were very cheap I could also afford to fail'.

The author of innumerable books, Messner is a former member of the European Parliament. In addition to his mountaineering and polar expeditions, he has made studies of the world's holy peaks and also the Yeti. In 2004, he crossed the Gobi desert. His current projects include the establishment of the Messner Mountain Museum.

CAPE EVANS, 1912
PATRICK KEOHANE 1879-1950

Born in County Cork, Petty Officer Keohane played a key role in the sledging journeys of Scott's *Terra Nova* expedition. He had joined the Royal Navy as a youth, rose to the rank of Petty Officer and was selected to join the voyage to Antarctica at the age of 30. After a spell as a coastguard, he would later rejoin the Navy and serve in the Second World War.

Strong and cheerful, Scott scribbled one of his favourites of Keohane's rhymes in his diary on the way south in 1911: 'The snow is all melting and everything's afloat / If this goes on much longer we shall have to turn the *tent* upside down and use it as a boat'. Keohane suffered snow blindness on the southern journey and on the way back to the hut at Cape Evans he fell down crevasses to the full length of his harness eight times in twenty-five minutes. In pleasing understatement, his companion Cherry-Garrard wrote that Keohane 'looked a bit dazed' after that ordeal.

Ponting captured this portrait on 29 January 1912, shortly after Keohane had returned from the treacherous 600-mile slog back from the Barrier to the safety of the hut. On 29 October, after spending the winter on the continent, Keohane was among the party that went to search for Scott's group. On 12 November they found the frozen bodies of Scott, Edward Wilson and Henry Bowers, eleven miles south of the One Ton supply depot.

LONDON, 2008
JANE NEDZHIPOVA 1982-

Turkish-Bulgarian Jane Nedzhipova doesn't want to be an explorer. Happy to be a popcorn seller, she works at the end of the street in North London where photographer Martin Hartley has his home; a place he rarely has the chance to spend much time.

Jane loves her Inuit-style fur parka, but can't see the appeal of the polar regions. 'Why would I want to go there', she replied, when asked if explorers were glamorous figures, 'the farthest north I have been is Birmingham, and that wasn't so great'.

LONDON, 1910
KATHLEEN SCOTT 1878-1947

After the *Discovery* expedition, Scott returned to sea duty and in 1908 became Flag Captain of HMS *Bulwark*. In September of that year he married Kathleen, daughter of Canon Lloyd Bruce, at Hampton Court Chapel. The following year, Scott went to the Admiralty as Naval Assistant to the Second Sea Lord and in September Kathleen and Scott's only child, Peter, was born.

Kathleen's early life had been a swirl of fashionable bohemia, attending the Slade School of Fine Art before escaping to Paris, the Académie Colarossi, and a sea of admirers. She was befriended by Auguste Rodin, whose influence can be seen in some of her early sculptures. She made a triumphant return to London society, where her close circle included James Barrie, George Bernard Shaw and Henry James.

She met Scott in 1906, and though their early courtship was marked by considerable doubt and anxiety, she was soon certain of her love for him. Their brief marriage was marked by lengthy separations because of his naval duties and from 1910 his fateful expedition. This rare portrait, her husband's favourite, was taken shortly before he left for Antarctica. Scott had two versions of this photograph pinned beside his bed in the hut at Cape Evans.

RESOLUTE BAY, 2003
PEN HADOW 1962-

Rupert Nigel Pendrill Hadow, educated at Harrow, has become one of the leading polar adventurers of his generation. A hugely experienced guide, 'Pen' was one of the first to enable people from all walks of life to make expeditions to the most remote places of the polar world. He made a series of bold expeditions of his own in the high Arctic in the 1990s, culminating in three extreme solo journeys on the Arctic Ocean. Founding the Polar Travel Company, he dedicated himself, despite some opposition in conservative circles, to opening up the Arctic to the adventure tourist. He was the organiser of the McVitie's Penguin Polar Relay, the first all-women novice expedition to the North Pole.

In 2003, Hadow became well known in Britain when he became the first man to sledge 478 miles from Canada to the North Pole without outside assistance – a feat of athleticism thought as hard as climbing Everest solo without oxygen. It had taken him three attempts, and over fifteen year's training, to achieve his goal. In 2004, Hadow guided 63-year old businessman Simon Murray to the South Pole, becoming the first Briton to walk without re-supply to both Poles, and all within twelve months.

This portrait shows Pen testing his immersion suit for the first time, in the Arctic waters of Resolute Bay, Cornwallis Island. He left on his daring solo expedition shortly afterward. On a soggy morning in 2007, standing waist deep in the waters of the Serpentine in Hyde Park, Hadow performed in his dry suit once more, before a handful of journalists and the flash of their cameras: part of the pageant of modern exploration. He was launching his ambitions for a new polar expedition. In 2009, he plans to make a journey across the Arctic Ocean surveying the state of the sea ice as he goes. He intends to haul a sledge with an innovative ice-penetrating impulse radar towed behind it. Raw data will be uplinked from a central onboard sledge computer, via the Iridium Satellite network, to scientific partners based at the University of Cambridge.

ANGMAGSSALIK, 1931
IKATEK 1906- n.d.

This unpublished portrait was taken during the British Arctic Air Route Expedition, an expedition which aimed to investigate the possibilities of an air route between England and Canada across the Arctic via Greenland, Baffin and Hudson Bay. The least-known part of the proposed route at that time was the east coast and central Ice Cap of Greenland. The team left St Katherine's Dock in London on 6 July 1930 in Shackleton's old ship *Quest*.

The expedition's official photographer was Flight-Lieutenant Iliffe Cozens, an RAF reserve pilot and filmmaker, but it is likely that this beautiful portrait was taken by Spencer Chapman, the artistic young ornithologist, probably sometime during March 1931 on the shores of Sermilik Sound.

Chapman was amazed by the skills of local Inuit hunters: 'Our Angmagssalik Eskimos, who can use a kayak in almost every month of the year, are probably the most accomplished kayakers in the world ... the kayak is not only a wonder of efficiency, but a veritable artistic triumph, a thing of infinite beauty. When the *Quest* first reached Greenland, we saw the natives in their kayaks throwing their harpoons with consummate grace; and later we saw them, dressed in waterproof coats, rolling the kayak right over in the water'.

ELLESMERE ISLAND, 2007

IAN WESLEY 1964-

Wesley's first experience of snow and ice was at the age of 16, in the Alps, when a friend fell on Mount Blanc. He had to sleep out for two nights in a snow-hole before a helicopter could lift them out. Born in 1964 on the Gower Peninsula, South Wales, where he spent much of his childhood sea-kayaking and climbing, Wesley graduated in Engineering from Bristol University. He travelled the world for two years before teaching mathematics in London. He moved to Dartmoor in 1994, where he met the polar guide Pen Hadow. He continues to enjoy travel and adventure – he has climbed Aconcagua and once drove the Plymouth to Dakar Rally in a £100 car.

A self-confessed 'gadgeteer, kit freak and outdoor enthusiast', Wesley provided support for Hadow's Solo North Pole expedition in 2003. He was also the base manager for an expedition by the British adventurer Ann Daniels. This portrait was taken at Eureka Weather Station, Ellesmere Island. Wesley is currently helping develop and test the scientific and communications equipment for the Arctic Survey, an ambitious journey to the Pole set to begin early in 2009. 'I think I'm out of place amongst the 'proper' Arctic types', he joked, when told that his portrait was going to appear in this book; 'You sure it's me?'

CAPE EVANS, 1912
CECIL MEARES 1877-1937

The son of an army officer of County Mayo, Meares was made of adventurous stuff. Before venturing into the Antarctic, he had travelled widely, fighting with the Scottish Horse in the Boer War and trading furs in Siberia. Intriguing and eccentric, he was something of a global adventurer. On the *Terra Nova* expedition, Meares was in charge of the dogs until he left the expedition in 1912, at the same time as his good friend Ponting. Edward Wilson found him 'typically a man of action and a most entertaining mess-mate and full of fun'.

It is said that Ponting became interested in polar exploration after meeting Meares on a steamer to Shanghai in 1905. His enthusiasm for the polar regions was infectious. Ponting recounts their meeting: 'He had been having a roughish time during the Russo-Japanese war, and needed a holiday ... we came to an arrangement by which he came along with me to act as an interpreter and to assist me in my photographic work, and for the following six months we travelled together in Burma, India and Ceylon'.

Whilst on the Trans-Siberian railway in 1907, Ponting duly took with him Scott's first book, *The Voyage of Discovery*, and the rest is history. After the expedition, Ponting and Meares joined forces on the lecture circuit. Whilst Ponting was entertaining the crowds with his film at London's fashionable Philharmonic Hall, Meares embarked on a provincial tour, taking a case of the photographs with him. At the outbreak of World War I he joined the Royal Flying Corps and rose to the rank of Lieutenant Colonel, later settling with his wife in Canada. This portrait was taken at the moment the support party returned from the Barrier, late in January 1912.

QUEEN MAUD LAND, 1980

LADY VIRGINIA 'GINNY' FIENNES 1947-2004

The first woman to be awarded the Polar Medal, Lady Fiennes was also the first woman to join the UK's Antarctic Club in recognition of her research work for the British Antarctic Survey and Sheffield University. The brains behind some of the most ambitious polar expeditions in recent history, Lady Fiennes was also one of Britain's most experienced polar radio operators. 'She was not impressed by bureaucracy, never took no for an answer and, though slightly built, could make big men quake in their boots with a flash of her bright blue eyes'.

Born in West Sussex, Virginia Pepper became a passionate deep-sea diver and was recruited to work for the National Trust of Scotland. She trained at the Royal Aircraft Establishment and joined the Women's Royal Army Corps Territorials. She was only nine when she met Ran (Ranulph Fiennes), then an unruly 12-year-old, just arrived in a neighbouring village from South Africa; they married in 1970. Shortly before their wedding she organised the first ascent of the River Nile by hovercraft. In 1972 she devised a plan to circumnavigate the world along its polar axis and ten years later her Transglobe Expedition team became the first to reach both Poles, to cross Antarctica and the Arctic Ocean and navigate a northwest passage.

In the 1980s she moved to Exmoor and began to raise a herd of pedigree Aberdeen Angus cattle and a flock of black Welsh Mountain sheep, establishing one of the highest working farms in the South West of England. When she heard that Ran was to have five fingers amputated because of frostbite, she commented, 'Oh damn, now we'll be shorthanded on the farm'. Ginny was known to her many friends and godchildren for her gentleness, generosity and integrity. A modest person, she hated being in the spotlight and rarely took credit for her achievements.

In November 2003 she was found to be suffering from stomach cancer, diagnosed on the day after her husband returned from running seven marathons in seven days on seven continents, raising funds for the British Heart Foundation, four months after Ran himself had suffered a massive heart attack. As she fought till the end, she was also planning new expeditions. She died on 20 February 2004 and is much missed by the polar community.

PORTLAND, 1891
JOSEPHINE PEARY 1863-1955

The daughter of a professor at the Smithsonian Institution, Josephine Cecilia Diebitsch was born in Washington in 1863. In 1885, while attending dancing school she met the young Robert Peary, the future Rear Admiral and famous Arctic explorer. They married in 1888 and began a life of discovery together.

Josephine's eagerness to explore prompted her to join her husband on his second expedition to Greenland in 1891-92, becoming the first white woman to over-winter on an Arctic expedition. She was an active participant on the voyage, shooting game and making clothes for the men. This rare portrait was taken in a Portland studio in 1891, shortly before she left on this trip. She accompanied her husband to Greenland again in 1893 and during this time gave birth to a daughter, Marie Ahnighito Peary, less than thirteen degrees from the Pole. Marie was nicknamed 'Snow Baby' by their Inuit companions and an American public who embraced them upon their return. Her daughter's middle name honoured the Inuit woman who made her first fur suit.

The Pearys had another child together, a son, Robert Edwin Peary Jr. During the Arctic expeditions, both Peary and his fellow explorer Matthew Henson fathered children with Inuit women. Josephine and Marie made another voyage to Greenland in 1897. In 1900, when her vessel, the *Windward*, was damaged by an iceberg, she spent the winter in Greenland some 300 miles south of her husband's camp. She had to endure a winter in the ice with his Inuit mistress. 'You will have been surprised, perhaps annoyed, to hear I came up on a ship', she wrote to her husband, 'but believe me had I known how things were with you I should not have come'. No matter how much his infidelity must have pained her, Josephine remained supportive of her husband.

After he returned from the Pole in 1909, the Pearys spent most of their time at their summer home on Eagle Island, off Harpswell in Casco Bay. After his death in 1920, she settled into a permanent home in Portland, enjoying time with her children and grandchildren. In 1955 the National Geographic Society awarded her its highest honour, the Medal of Achievement. Josephine was buried in Arlington National Cemetery alongside her husband, as a mark of honour in tribute to her inspirational 'courage and devotion'.

RESOLUTE BAY, 2003
GARY GUY 1950-

Now semi-retired and living in the south, Gary Guy was something of a 'local legend' when he lived up in Resolute. If you needed something fixed, then Guy was your man. In fact, he was the man to ask if you needed *anything* repaired, ordered, borrowed or purloined. Guy moved to the Arctic as an electrician working for the Nunavut Power Corporation, whilst also offering his considerable skills as an outfitter for polar expeditions. If you needed a drink, he was also a good man to know. Much-loved by the Inuit locals, and by visiting travellers, it is said that Guy used to order his beer once a year from mainland Canada. It arrived by ship and took up the space of a container lorry.

In 2001, two years after the creation of Canada's Nunavut Territory, the Nunavut Power Corporation was established to oversee electricity provision. Although hydro-electric options are being investigated at a number of sites around Iqaluit, most communities are now heavily reliant on independent diesel power generators, fueled by re-supply during the summer shipping season. Severe weather, remoteness and expensive technologies make long-distance high voltage grids unviable. In 2002, the state-controlled company was renamed Quilliq Energy Corporation – drawing its name from the blubber candle lamp and stove used by generations of Inuit for heat and light – with a mandate to pursue energy conservation and alternative energy sources in the face of spiralling fuel costs.

ROSS ICE SHELF, 1929
ARTHUR WALDEN 1871-1947

The son of a Boston minister, the young Arthur Treadwell Walden rushed north to Alaska, where he joined other prospectors in the gold fields of the Klondike. Whilst in the Yukon, he learned to drive a team of heavyweight mongrels and, returning to his New Hampshire farm in 1900, began breeding and training a new type of 'half-husky' sled dog. In establishing the first East International Dog Derby in 1922, he gave rise to a popular sport. In 1924, he founded the New England Sled Dog Club, which is still in operation today.

Walden heard of Rear Admiral Richard Byrd's plans for a major Antarctic voyage and at 56 years - though way beyond the specified age limit – he applied to join the expedition. He got the job and spent the following year assembling equipment and training dogs and drivers at his 1300-acre farm in Wonalancet. In 1928, Walden, a team of 9 drivers and 97 dogs left for Antarctica, where they were chiefly employed in shifting supplies from ship to their base, 'Little America'.

'Had it not been for the dogs', Byrd later wrote, 'our attempts to conquer the Antarctic by air must have ended in failure ... Walden's team was the backbone of our transport. Seeing him rush his heavy loads along the trail, outstripping the younger men, it was difficult to believe that he was an old man. He was 58 years old, but he had the determination and strength of youth'. He returned from Antarctica in 1930, greatly in debt. He devoted much of his later life to writing books and caring for his wife. He died in 1947, overcome by smoke inhalation after a fire broke out in his farmhouse, having rescued his wife from the flames.

PATRIOT HILLS, 2003
JACO WIUM 1967-

Jaco Wium has possibly the most stressful job in Antarctica. He is the weatherman at Patriot Hills and he alone has to make the decision whether planes can take off at Punta Arenas and land on the continent. Weather can change dramatically in moments. If an aircraft has to turn back, or an error is made, it can cost more than £140,000 in fuel. If a drastic error is made, it can cost the lives of those onboard.

This is an unenviable job, perhaps, sitting in a tent all season coping with the daily mix of excitement, boredom, frustration and anxiety: 'Instead of being outdoors, *in the wind* for long periods of time – after all, shouldn't a weatherman also be a *weathered* man? – I had to sit and listen to the tent walls being battered and shaken instead'. Yet, the modest South African handles his job with a calm assurance. 'Stressful ... yes, of course', he jokes, 'can't you see, it's enough to make you lose your hair!'

We asked Jaco to describe this portrait: 'I'm thrilled to be associated in a book with such legends of the polar world; well, here goes ... this shot captures me during a prolonged period of watching dials and numbers in an effort to establish trends in the current weather. Due to the camp's proximity to the Ellsworth Mountain Range and the katabatic flow of air from the polar plateau, the winds often behave very erratically, so it is a skill to distinguish between temporary breaks in a storm, and a period of good weather settling in. All aircraft operations depend on being sure of the latter'.

'Antarctica is, to most people, a dead place. Yet for any active observer, or anyone else who has tuned into the glacial rhythms of that awesome continent, it is constantly moving, constantly changing ... however subtle or dramatic. As sailors on the ocean, and dwellers of sandy deserts can testify, there is never a dull moment. Antarctica is where I feel truly at home. Frankly speaking, Antarctica is the love of my life'.

WHITE SEA, 1932
LUDOLF SCHJELDERUP 1894-1983

Shackleton's final Antarctic expedition, the apparent objective of which was to circumnavigate the continent, seemed to have been driven more than anything else by the explorer's desire to get away, drawn by the empty embrace of the southern oceans. Shackleton bought a ship in poor condition in Norway, a creaky wooden sealer called the *Foca 1*, and had it refitted in London. He renamed her *Quest* and sailed on 17 September 1921, leaving England for the last time.

In 1930, *Quest* was chartered by the British Arctic Air Route Expedition and its experienced master Captain Schjelderup took charge of the Norwegian crew. During their voyage to the east coast of Greenland, his abilities and bravado earned him wide admiration from the young Cambridge University graduates and their leader George 'Gino' Watkins. 'Usually the *Quest* anchored from 9.30pm till 2am, when it got too dark to make out sunken rocks and hidden dangers ahead; but now, with violent gusts of wind and rain heralding no common storm, the Captain boldly smashed through the ice in the half-light with his engines at full speed. It was on such occasions that Captain Schjelderup – who always donned his bowler hat when things became really serious – seemed to enjoy himself to the full'.

The men awoke the following morning, after the storm had subsided, to find the ship safe at anchor at the head of a fjord, which was not even marked on the map. In the distance they could make out the Captain, with an Inuk companion, their trousers rolled up to their knees, gleefully netting salmon on a shallow sandbank. Schjelderup's portrait shown here – proudly posing with armfuls of seal pups – was taken in 1932 during a voyage in the White Sea.

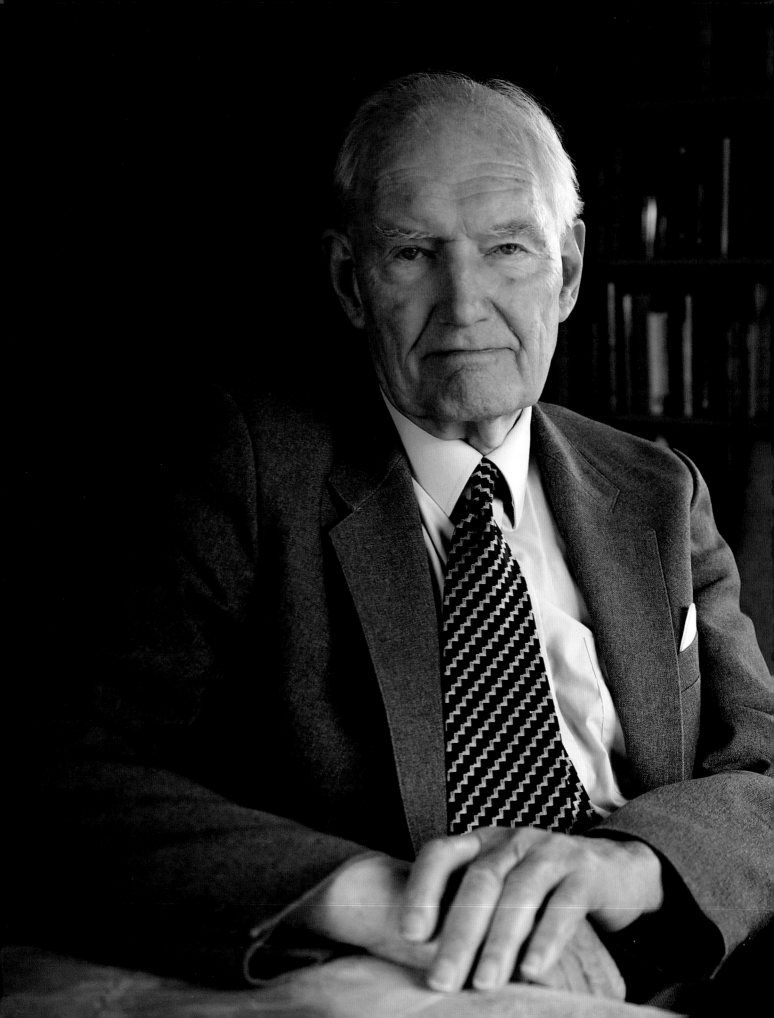

CAMBRIDGE, 2008
CHARLES SWITHINBANK 1926-

Born in 1926, in Pegu, Burma, Charles Swithinbank was a sub-lieutenant in the RNVR during the Second World War, serving in a cruiser, an aircraft carrier and a minesweeper. In 1947 he joined the Oxford University expedition to Vatnajökull in Iceland and in 1948, an expedition to Gambia. The youngest member of the Norwegian-British-Swedish Antarctic Expedition, 1949-52, Swithinbank completed his studies at Oxford a few months before leaving for the South.

Swithinbank has dedicated his life to polar research. He spent four years studying the distribution of pack ice in Canadian and Greenlandic waters. He was aboard the supertanker SS *Manhattan* during her pioneering voyage through a northwest passage in 1969 and later accompanied the British nuclear submarine HMS *Dreadnought* to the North Pole in 1971. He has visited the South Pole on numerous occasions. He was Chief Glaciologist of the British Antarctic Survey from 1963 to 1974, then Head of Earth Sciences Division until 1986. A long-serving Senior Associate of the Scott Polar Research Institute, Swithinbank has also been President of the International Glaciological Society.

During a pre-eminent scientific career, Dr Swithinbank spent over 20 field seasons in the polar regions and since 'retiring' he continues to be involved in the interpretation of satellite images of Antarctica, mapping and the development of ice runways for support aircraft. This portrait was taken at his home in Cambridge.

WEDDELL SEA, 1915
REGINALD JAMES 1891-1964

Red-haired Reginald 'Jimmy' James, his fringe flecked with snowflakes, was perhaps stereotypical of the sheltered academic. Shy and baffled in company, he was brilliant in his field. The son of an umbrella maker, he excelled at Cambridge and had given up an impressive university appointment at the Cavendish Laboratory to go south. In London, Shackleton interviewed the young graduate in order to complete his scientific staff. James later recalled their first meeting: 'All that I can clearly remember of it is that I was asked if I had good teeth, if I suffered from varicose veins, and if I could sing'.

Reserved and almost always earnestly devoted to his work, he was often the target for light-hearted teasing onboard *Endurance*. 'James was a physicist, and was engaged in working magnetic observations, occultations of stars', described one of his shipmates. 'He had some wonderful electrical machines which none of us understood, and a joke of ours that annoyed him very much, was that he did not either'.

After the expedition James joined the war effort, serving at Ypres with the Royal Engineers, calculating positions of the enemy's guns by monitoring sound using microphone surveillance. He was mentioned in despatches. After the war, he became an expert in x-ray crystallography. To the astonishment of his friends, he married a Manchester headmistress and moved to South Africa, where he was appointed Professor of Physics and later Principal at Cape Town University.

PATRIOT HILLS, 2003
GARY MIDDLETON 1975-

Gary Middleton is a polar mechanic. Some years his 'day job' is at Rothera, the British Antarctic Survey research base on Adelaide Island, 1,860km south of the Falklands. This summer, Gary is working for Antarctic Logistics and Expeditions at Patriot Hills to prepare the runway and to keep all the heavy equipment at the base operational. That includes bulldozers, skidoos, oil-powered heaters, cookers, boilers, fuel pumps and even chainsaws (for digging out ice caves for storage underground).

The first days of the season are the hardest, because the small start-up team has to build the camp and clear the runway so that the first Ilyushin flight can come in from Chile. Getting to Patriot Hills from Punta Arenas in a Twin Otter is a long two-days flying, with hours of work to change the undercarriage from wheels to skis at a re-fuelling stop en route. Upon landing at Patriot, Gary's first job is to get all the engines started that have been sitting on the runway during the long, cold Antarctic winter, in temperatures well below -40 degrees for most of that time. 'He keeps the whole place moving', a friend says. 'Spare a thought for Gary next time you moan about the cold, when your car won't start on a chilly November morning!'

He stands beside a Tucker Snocat vehicle, used for all sorts of work at the base, in which he had driven to rescue a polar guide who had sliced his thumb open whilst trying to cut some frozen cheese. Behind Gary is the Bell B407 helicopter that the remarkable Jennifer Murray had just flown to the South Pole. Not long after this photograph was taken Gary was airborne himself, flying in a Twin Otter to rescue Murray, who had crashed her helicopter in white-out conditions.

TORONTO, 1882
JOHN CHEYNE 1826-1902

Commander John Powles Cheyne, showman-explorer, is captured in a studio portrait in 1882. He was in North America trying to raise funds for an expedition to the North Pole by balloon. When he arrived in New York, journalists described his appearance: 'The Commander, although over fifty years of age and with whitened hair, yet looks and is strong and hardy and possesses much more vigor than many men ten or fifteen years his junior. He is a little below the medium height, but with a well knit frame, complexion ruddy, penetrating eyes of gray, and wears small white whiskers'.

A veteran of three Arctic expeditions in search of the missing Franklin party, Cheyne was also a keen amateur photographer and began to experiment with photography in the 1850s. After the return of his former mess-mate Francis McClintock in 1859, Cheyne photographed him surrounded by the relics of the Franklin expedition. He sold sets of the novel stereoviews from his London home.

His life after retirement from the Royal Navy was an unusual one. After a number of failed business ventures, Cheyne became a journeyman lecturer, probably the first polar explorer to turn professional performer. From 1876 he became convinced that he could fly a balloon to the North Pole and he gave innumerable lectures in Britain and North America in an effort to raise funds for his scheme. Proving unable to win over a rightly sceptical public – many thought him a madman, dubbing his plans 'balloonacy' – Cheyne was unable to realise his dream of polar flight. He died in 1902, just a few days after Captain Scott ascended in a balloon above the Ross Ice Shelf on the *Discovery* expedition, becoming the first man to fly over Antarctica.

KESWICK, 2008
GEOFF SOMERS 1956-

Geoff Somers is one of Britain's most accomplished polar travellers. He has completed several 'Firsts', including the only traverse of the entire Antarctic Continent by its greatest axis – a seven-month, almost 6,200 km journey, using husky dogs to pull the sledges. To train for this expedition, his team traversed some 2,000km of the Greenland Ice Cap from south to north. During both of these adventures, Somers was responsible for the logistics, navigation and driving the lead team of husky dogs.

On foot, on ski and by kite power, he has travelled some 22,500 km in the Arctic and Antarctic. He has been six times to the South Pole and six times, leading groups, to the North Pole. Somers has also worked in Outward Bound schools throughout the world. As deputy director, he helped set up the Outward Bound school in Sabah Malaysia and, amongst other rainforest journeys, he crossed Borneo through untravelled jungle. In Australia, with three camels from the wild, he travelled from Perth across the deserts to Uluru, the 'Red Centre' of this remarkable continent. He is photographed here at his home in the Lake District. 'Here are three variations on my CV', he said, when asked it if we could feature him in this book: 'I feel small fry compared with the others on your prestigious line up! Pick out the bits that you want. If you don't like them, let me know!'

Somers now spends most of his time lecturing about his experiences, at motivational business seminars, to packed village halls, or on cruise ships plying their way amongst the ice. Hartley first met Somers at a lecture he was giving in London. The young photographer asked him how he kept his cameras working in challenging polar conditions. The secret, Somers revealed, was to wrap them in a towel, and then in a plastic bag if brought inside the tent, which helps stops condensation ruining the camera. This simple advice has served Hartley well on many trips since.

GREENLAND, 1906
ALF TROLLE 1879-1949

Captain Trolle took over command of the *Danmark* expedition, 1906-08, after the tragic death of its leader Ludvig Mylius-Erichsen, and sailed the sealing-steamer home to Copenhagen. On this expedition, great swathes of unknown coastline of Northeast Greenland were charted and gigantic new fjords discovered over a series of epic sledge journeys totalling more than 4,000 miles.

Misled by existing maps, Mylius-Erichsen, with his companions Peter Høeg-Hagen and Jørgen Brønlund, had travelled so far from their ship that return was impossible and they perished from starvation, debilitating frostbite and exhaustion, attempting to reach safety. Brønlund's diary was later recovered: 'I perished under the hardships of the return journey over the inland ice in November. I reached this place under a waning moon, and cannot go on because of my frozen feet and the darkness. The bodies of the others are somewhere in the middle of the fjord'. The remains of his companions have never been found.

Trolle later travelled to London to present the harrowing news, in person, to the Royal Geographical Society. He was met with genuine sympathy and was commended by the Danish Ambassador, to huge applause, as being one of the country's 'brave sons'. In 1933, the twenty-fifth anniversary of the return of the expedition, Trolle set up a fund to support members of the expedition and their dependants, and to further the exploration of East Greenland through grants to expeditions for their work and for the publication of scientific results.

KINGUSSIE, 2008

ALLAN GILL 1930-

On 6 April 1969, Wally Herbert and his companions Allan Gill, Roy Koerner and Ken Hedges of the British Trans-Arctic Expedition, without any doubt became the first men to reach the North Pole on foot. They had spent most of the previous day trying to get an accurate fix on the elusive spot, as they drifted on the shifting sea ice; an experience Herbert described as 'trying to step on the shadow of a bird that was circling overhead'. The team continued on to complete the first surface crossing of the Arctic Ocean by its longest axis – Barrow, Alaska to Svalbard – a feat that has never been repeated.

Gill was photographed in Scotland, where he is now living. Though in poor health, the veteran explorer still managed to raise a smile and share some good stories about his travels. At the North Pole that day, almost forty years ago, Gill had set up the camera as the team posed for their pictures – thirty-six shots at different exposures. 'We tried not to look weary', Herbert described, 'tried not to look cold; tried only to huddle, four fur-clad figures, in a pose that was vaguely familiar – for what other proof could we bring back that we had reached the Pole?' Today, Gill has a photo of this North Pole triumph in his room, by his bed. There is great comfort in recollection.

Gill began his polar career on British bases in the Antarctic. He had gone South at the same time as Koerner, and the pair went on a number of expeditions together in the Canadian Arctic. On Koerner's advice, Herbert travelled to the Arctic Institute of North America in 1965 to meet Gill, who was then preparing for an expedition to Devon Island. 'I remember very well my first impression of Gill', he recalled, 'a deeply creased, parchment-faced, wiry individual – the scruffiest man in the Institute'. A 'master of temporary repair and ingenious contraptions', Gill had already spent three winters in the Antarctic, one in the Canadian Arctic and two on the Arctic Ocean at the American scientific drifting station T-3. Herbert and Gill became loyal friends. 'Here was a man who clearly was ideally suited for the sort of expedition I was planning', Herbert wrote, 'a tough man of placid temperament who loved the polar environment and could make an invaluable contribution as a trained geophysical observer'.

Later, in 1978-79, Herbert and Gill made the first attempt to circumnavigate Greenland with dog sledge and skin boat. Herbert described how they were caught in hurricane-force winds: 'that blizzard raged for 36 hours and by the time it had blown itself out, Allan and I were near total wrecks. For that 36 hours we had not been able to speak to each other because of the noise of the flapping tent, which had also given us splitting headaches and had made it impossible to light the stove, or to have anything to eat or drink. We had no choice but to sit there shivering – convinced by the reflected fear that we could see in each other's eyes that we had only minutes to live. Small wonder then that when the wind finally eased enough for us to be able to shout above it, the first words spoken were: 'never again', 'never, ever again!"

GRYTVIKEN, 1914

FRANK WORSLEY 1872-1943

Possibly no man is more responsible for the safe return of the crews of Shackleton's *Endurance* expedition than her New Zealand captain Frank Arthur Worsley. A man whose incredible charisma was matched by erratic eccentricity, 'The Skipper' was much liked by his men: he enjoyed shocking his shipmates by taking snow baths on the ice. 'He is a vital spark', wrote a shipmate, 'his activity and keenness are extraordinary'. He was, above all, a master sailor and a peerless navigator.

Hurley took this photograph at anchor off Grytviken whaling station in 1914, shortly before Endurance headed south into the heavy pack of the Weddell Sea. Writing in his diary on 24 January 1915, Worsley was impressed by the adventurous young photographer: 'Hurley the irrepressible ... is taking a colour photo of the ship and ice ... he is a marvel – with cheerful Australian profanity he perambulates alone aloft and everywhere, in the most dangerous and slippery places he can find, content and happy at all times but cursing so if he can get a good or novel picture. Stands bare [headed] and hair waving in the wind, where we are gloved and helmeted, he snaps his snap or winds his handle turning out curses of delight and pictures of Life by the fathom'.

Worsley's skills were put to the test so many times on the *Endurance* voyage, but nowhere more obviously than during the 800-mile open boat journey to South Georgia, where even the slightest navigational error would have meant the difference between life and death. Worsley later served in the First World War commanding anti-submarine boats. He also captained Shackleton's last expedition ship, *Quest*, in 1921-22. In 1925 he became joint leader of an Arctic expedition to Franz Joseph Land and in 1935 was part of an expedition to the Cocos Islands in search of treasure. He continued to instruct at the Royal Naval College in Greenwich until his death in 1943. His ashes were scattered at sea near the mouth of the River Thames.

KHATANGA, 2004
RUSSIAN MAN 1953-

It was cold that day, but nothing out of the ordinary. It hadn't been above −42 degrees in Khatanga for the previous two weeks. Hartley was hanging around in the town square, looking for people to photograph. He saw this man trudging towards him through the biting cold. They exchanged a smile. He thrust his hands back into his pockets and continued on his way down the street.

Khatanga is a small fishing village in the Taymyr Peninsula, on the edge of the Arctic Ocean. It is one of the most northerly habitations in Russia. The area is often visited by Western tourists, using it as an entry point into the Siberian wilderness and it is also used as a base by aspiring polar adventurers looking to the North Pole. Amenities in Khatanga include a hotel, an airport, a small natural history museum and weather reporting stations. Vodka is essential.

ROSS ICE SHELF, 1929
RICHARD BYRD 1888-1957

Discharged from active service in the US Navy due to leg injuries, Richard Byrd took to the air: 'My one chance of escape from a life of inaction', he later declared, 'was to learn to fly'. On 9 May 1926 he made an airborne attempt at the North Pole and claimed huge success, but later evidence suggests that he was well short of his goal. His fiercest critics claimed that he merely flew in circles once he was out of sight. In November 1929, however, he became the first person to fly to the South Pole and five years later he led another expedition to Antarctica. In this remarkable unpublished portrait, we see Byrd taking a shave, having just returned to safety.

His second expedition was a success too, remarkable now for two things above all: its comprehensive survey of large tracts of unknown ice cap; and for Byrd's bizarre insistence on wintering alone on the Antarctic plateau. 'Out there on the South Polar barrier', he said, 'I should have time to catch up, to study and think ... to live exactly as I choose, obedient to no necessities but those imposed by wind and night and cold, and to no man's laws but my own'. Within a few months he was poisoned by carbon monoxide from a poorly-ventilated generator. His sickness continued and eventually he had to radio for help, putting in danger those men who aborted several missions before finally rescuing him.

Byrd's fondness for publicity earned him a reputation as a sensation-seeker, but by the end of his life he was respected as an elder statesman of polar affairs. His lasting achievement was to have pressed for Antarctica to become a zone of international cooperation.

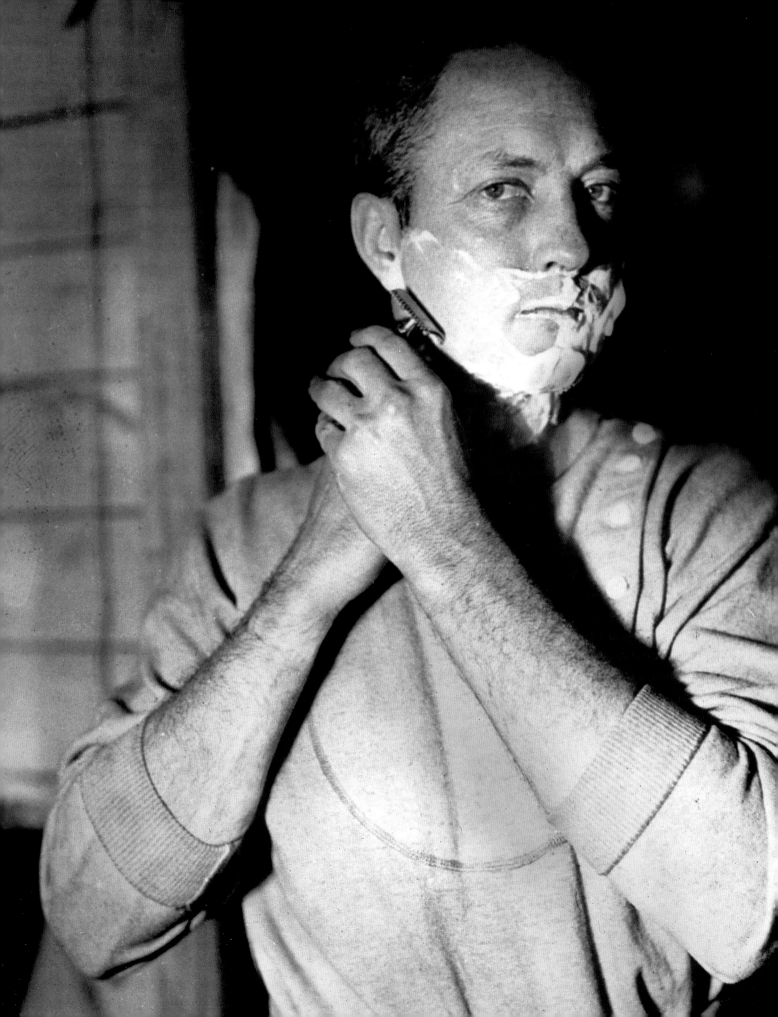

CAMBRIDGE, 2008
PHIL COATES 1966-

Coates is an extremely versatile and experienced photographer and altitude filmmaker, who began his polar career as a British Antarctic Survey field assistant on the island of Signy. 'If you are shooting at −38°C or 7,900 metres, with the pressure of a million-pound budget, whilst juggling your camera and sound equipment, missing the action is never really an option', he jokes over a cup of tea at his home in Cambridge.

It is something of a rarity to find him here, as his work takes him far from the Fens. He was the cameraman/producer/director on the Anglo-Australian expedition to the Magnetic North Pole in 1998, and has travelled with his camera on expeditions all over the globe: among temples in Bhutan, on multiple crossings of Greenland, through the Tian Shan Mountains in the borders of Kazakhstan, to following in the footsteps of Mallory in Tibet.

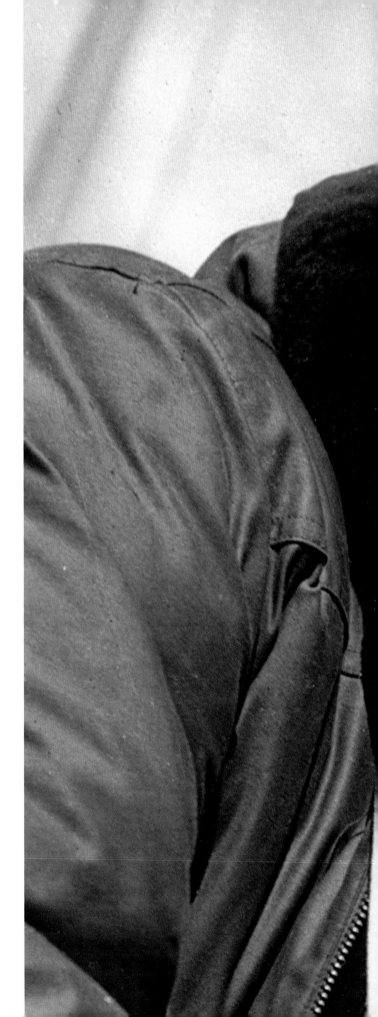

DISKO BAY, 1948
PAUL-ÉMILE VICTOR 1907-1995

Paul-Émile Victor, or 'PEV' to his friends, was a French explorer and ethnologist who spent over five decades documenting the earth's polar wildernesses in countless books, paintings and scientific papers. From his first visit to Greenland with Jean Charcot, as a young man in 1934, to his last expedition to Antarctica in 1987, it is estimated he covered almost 312,000 miles in the polar regions. Yet, he was the first to declare that he absolutely hated the cold and wind, snow and ice.

In 1947, he founded the Expéditions Polaires Françaises and by his retirement in 1976 had led more than 3,000 people on scientific expeditions to both poles. He was a tireless campaigner for the protection of wildlife and for the autonomy of indigenous groups, in particular the Inuit. With the French oceanographer and explorer Jacques-Yves Cousteau, he set up an association in 1974 to protect man and his environment, known as the Group Paul-Émile Victor.

An enigmatic public figure, Victor was energetic, handsome, impatient with those who lacked imagination, and spell-binding when performing before an audience at lectures or in his countless television documentaries. Victor presented this signed portrait – one of his favourites – to the Scott Polar Research Institute in 1961. Saying he wanted a calm place to write and paint, Victor moved to the warmth of the Pacific in 1977 with his second wife, Colette and their daughter. He died in 1995 on a South Pacific island in French Polynesia. His body was taken on a frigate of the French navy and entrusted to the deep, in the warm waters of the Bora-Bora lagoon that he knew and loved so well.

SEVERNAYA ZEMLYA, 2008
ANATOLY OMELCHENKO 1961-

Severnaya Zemlya is an archipelago in the Russian high Arctic, lying in ice-choked waters off Siberia's Taymyr Peninsula. The island group was only charted for the first time in 1933, making it the last archipelago on Earth to be discovered. It is certainly remote. Around 18,300km of Severnaya Zemlya is permanently covered in ice. Mean annual temperatures hover around −16°C, with temperatures regularly dropping below minus 40 degrees. October Revolution Island is the largest of the group, and over half is covered with glaciers reaching down to the sea. During the Cold War a station was established at nearby Sredniy Island, with a runway designed for use by long-range bombers in the event of war.

The Golomyanniy Meteorological Station is located at the northernmost tip of Sredniy, and at 79°33'N this small outpost is one of the most northerly settlements in the world. It has been taking continuous measurements since 1954. The station is run by two couples who work for 7 days a week, 365 days a year for two years, after which one of the couples takes six months leave in rotation. Anatoly Omelchenko, a scientist and mechanic, lives at the base with his wife Svetlana. This portrait was taken after a dinner at the weather station. Hartley describes the scene: 'Antaloy took me into his workshop to show me some kind of trick with a welding torch, smoking as he went. Luckily the gas ran out before he could show me what the trick was!'

SCOTIA SEA, 1950
GUTTORM JAKOBSEN 1910-n.d.

In this rare portrait, Captain Guttorm Jakobsen has been photographed on the bridge of *Norsel*, the ship that supported the Norwegian-British-Swedish Antarctic Expedition of 1949-52. It was a tremendously successful expedition – the first in Antarctica involving an international team of scientists – and its legacy of international cooperation survives to this day. Norway was mainly responsible for meteorology and topographical surveys, Britain for geology and Sweden for glaciology.

Norsel was a 700-ton ocean-going tug, an unfinished war relic, refitted for polar service in Germany. Jakobsen was an old school-fellow of the expedition's leader John Giæver, and he joined the ship as its captain as she lay at anchor in Oslo. '*Norsel* set out on her maiden voyage like a lively young filly, buoyant and gay, fresh in her coat of gleaming white', Giæver later wrote, describing one of Jakobsen's morning meditations at the helm. 'But now she is more pitilessly overladen than a donkey of Arabia, and she lumbers along with the heavy motions of a sow. For that matter, she is just as dirty too and smells even worse. May the weather-gods of the Antarctic have mercy upon us!'

Jakobsen went to sea at the age of 15 and learnt his trade as a sealing skipper. He became one of Norway's foremost master mariners during the Second World War, earning both an OBE and Lloyd's medal for bravery. 'Typically, he frowned with the distant look of a sailor, but this was only because he chose not to wear sunglasses'. He rarely left the bridge of his ship, save to take his meals in the crew's mess, and he was almost always seen smoking, with binoculars to hand, searching for hunting grounds or fresh leads in the ice. Over a long career it is said he spent some 50 seasons in the Arctic Ocean, an incomparable record in polar waters.

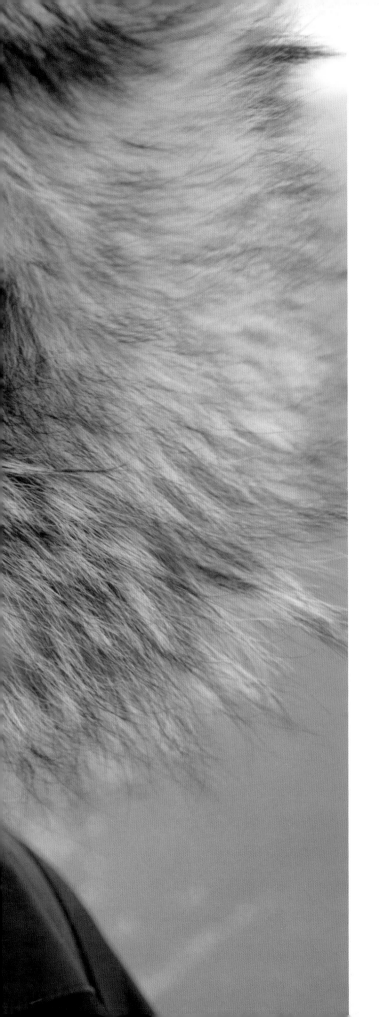

BARNEO BASE, 2006
ALAIN HUBERT 1953-

Belgian-born Alain Hubert is a polar traveller of formidable and wide-ranging talents. He is photographed here at Barneo, a camp established on the Arctic sea ice each year about 100km from the North Pole. Once a civil engineer, now author, environmentalist, entrepreneur, mountain guide and Goodwill Ambassador for UNICEF, Hubert's career has been impressive. In a recent interview for *National Geographic Adventure*, Hubert described his interests: 'Because of reading certain books when I was young, one of my dreams was to go to the polar regions. When I was about 38, I said to myself, why don't you try to live your dream? So I decided to go to the North Pole; then the South Pole. One day I was crossing the street in the center of Brussels and I saw two young kids playing like two young explorers right there in the street. One of them said to the other – Hey, Alain, pull your sledge! – I was totally impressed. On this particular day, I decided to do more'.

Hubert has climbed in some of the harshest mountain environments in the world, including Everest, Kangchenjunga, Cho Oyu, the Pamirs and Antarctica's Queen Maud Land. In 1997-98, he travelled across Antarctica for some 3,924km in just 99 days – using innovative new power kites – in a remarkable demonstration of skill, strength and, not least, preparation. In 2002, with Dr André Berger, a climatologist at the Université Catholique de Louvain, and Dr Hugo Decleir, glaciologist at the Vrije Universiteit Brussel, Hubert co-founded the International Polar Foundation (IPF), a charitable non-profit organisation established to disseminate polar research and to educate the wider public about the ongoing impact of human actions on the polar world.

For his commitment to raising environmental awareness, in 2008 Hubert was awarded the inaugural 'Climate Change Prize' by the Fondation Prince Albert II de Monaco. The IPF is currently engaged in building a series of Polaris Climate Change Observatories, with the first to be situated in Brussels. The observatory's main objective will be to make climate change comprehensible for the general public – while focusing on the importance of polar science in understanding its causes and consequences. Hubert has also assisted with the Princess Elisabeth Base, due to be finished by the end of 2008, which promises to be the first-ever 'zero emission' polar research station.

LONDON, 1914
GEORGE MARSTON 1882-1940

The official artist on both the *Nimrod* and *Endurance* voyages, Marston was also a gifted author, singer and amateur actor. On the latter expedition he was 'in charge of the clothing and general equipment', which included the sledges and the huts. From his days as a student at the Regent Street Polytechnic, he was a good friend of Shackleton's sister Kathleen. '*Mind* you do your *own* style of work', she wrote before he departed for the south. 'Don't mind Ernest. He knows nothing about Art'.

He was known to the crew as 'Putty', for his mobile facial features, and by his family as 'Muffin'. Raymond Priestley, a shipmate on the *Nimrod*, described Marston as having the 'frame and face of a prize-fighter and the disposition of a fallen angel'. He was certainly very tough, but also had a sensitive soul that endeared him to others. Shackleton was keen to recruit Marston again and the artist was one of the first people he signed up, being promised a salary of £350 per year. This quite remarkable fur-clothing costume was used only for this publicity photograph, taken before the expedition sailed in 1914. He is perhaps best remembered for surrendering his beloved oil paints to help caulk the seams of the *James Caird* to make it watertight, shortly before its epic 800-mile open sea voyage in search of rescue.

In later life Marston went on to work very hard in the cause of handicrafts and rural industries in Hampshire. Marston lost most of his pictures when *Endurance* sank beneath the ice, but brought back many sketches from Elephant Island, which he later worked up. Though a fire in his home destroyed much of his work, a number of his paintings survive in the collections of the Scott Polar Research Institute.

IGLOOLIK, 2005
GRAHAM DICKSON 1975-

Graham Dickson is the founder and Chief Expedition Officer for Toronto-based Arctic Kingdom Marine Expeditions, the world's leading company for managing complicated logistics in the Far North. The company started out running diving expeditions for adventurers and film crews and expanded into supporting scientific, engineering and mining operations. Dickson has been diving for almost two decades and is now a Master Instructor, certainly one of the most experienced working in the polar regions today.

He led the first sport diving expedition to Nunavut to dive with walrus in 1999 and has since led multiple expeditions for Bowhead whales, narwhals, belugas, polar bear and the Greenland shark. He has also led expeditions across most of the Arctic from Alaska to the Northwest Passage, Hudson's Bay to the Foxe Basin and from Greenland to Svalbard, employing a variety of travel techniques: trusty dog teams, kayaks and snowmobiles, large zodiacs deployed from Twin Otter aircraft, chartered 727s, Hercules, Basler DC3s and helicopters. He was the first to use air-boats in the high Arctic for travel over thin pack ice.

Dickson leads everything from private one-on-one expeditions through large multiple-season projects with coordinated, simultaneous camps. Dickson is driven to find new regions and ways to access new areas of the Arctic safely, at times of the year previously inaccessible, by combining Inuit traditional knowledge with the latest cutting-edge technologies. Dickson builds expedition training programmes for Arctic Kingdom's large global network of professionals, who bring diverse and complementary skills together in the most remote corners of the Arctic. From tracked amphibious vehicles to infrared aerial imaging to underwater remote sensing, modern Arctic exploration embraces and combines cutting-edge transportation and scientific tools to take exploration to new heights and depths.

In 2007, Dickson was elected to the Board of Directors for Nunavut Tourism as the representative for ecotourism and adventure travel. He is trained in cave diving through the National Speleological Society (NSS-CDS), underwater archeology through the Nautical Archaeological Society (NAS) and is also a Medic First Aid/CPR Instructor and an accomplished ice-climbing guide. He has also authored multiple entries in *The Encyclopedia of the Arctic* and regularly contributes to *The Diving Almanac*. Dickson is a modest guy, who enjoys a pint in the pub, but is at his happiest when amongst the ice. He has an impressive polar CV, certainly more rounded than that of many other modern adventurers. He is a true polar professional.

F. G. Jackson
with hearty good wishes
from Fridtjof Nansen
15 August 1898

LONDON, 1898
FRIDTJOF NANSEN 1861-1930

In 1888, the young Norwegian Nansen abandoned a promising career as a neuroscientist in favour of becoming a polar explorer. He had obtained his doctorate four days before leaving for Greenland and in the autumn of 1889 he married the singer Eva Sars. He became the first to traverse Greenland by ski, and between 1893 and 1896 he made a record-breaking journey across the Arctic pack, carried by the currents in his revolutionary little ship *Fram*. After a daring ski dash for the Pole, Nansen reached 86°10' N before turning back for Franz Josef Land, where he spent the long winter in a stone hut. He had planned to paddle back to Norway by kayak but was instead rescued, by chance, by the British explorer Frederick Jackson. Nansen presented him with this portrait after they returned to safety.

Carefully planned, brilliantly executed, involving no loss of life (except the dogs'), and of enormous scientific benefit, this pioneering expedition changed the face of exploration. Nansen went on to enjoy an illustrious career and was both broadly skilled and widely admired, perhaps more than any explorer before or after him. Holding a research professorship at the University of Oslo after 1897, Nansen published six volumes of scientific observations made during this voyage and, continuing to break new ground

in research, was appointed Professor of Oceanography in 1908. In 1919, he became president of the Norwegian Union for the League of Nations and at the Peace Conference in Paris was an influential lobbyist for the rights of small nations. In the spring of 1920, the League of Nations asked him to undertake the task of repatriating prisoners of war, many of them held in Russia. Working with customary boldness and ingenuity, he repatriated over 450,000 prisoners in less than two years and later worked with the International Red Cross directing famine relief.

Nansen was awarded the Nobel Peace Prize in 1922. 'Perhaps what has most impressed all of us', the Chairman of the Nobel Committee declared, 'is his ability to stake his life time and time again on a single idea, on one thought, and to inspire others to follow him'. Enjoying international renown as a scientist, able diplomat and hero of polar exploration, Nansen may be best remembered as the altruistic champion of people in times of distress. He was busily engaged in making arrangements for an airship flight across the Arctic when he died suddenly of a heart attack in 1930, shortly before his 70th birthday. He was buried in a state funeral on 17 May, Norway's Independence Day.

LONDON, 2008
HUGH BRODY 1943 -

Professor Hugh Brody is an acclaimed writer, anthropologist and filmmaker. His award-winning reflection on the human condition, *The Other Side of Eden*, was born from years of living and working with the peoples of the Arctic. 'Nobody – *nobody* – writes better about the northern reaches of our planet', declared one typical review of this beautiful book. 'Brody is absolutely fearless in his thinking, bold in his writing, generous in his knowledge and love of existence itself'.

'The thing about being with the Inuit', Brody says over a cup of tea at his home in London, as his portrait was taken, 'is that you have a sense of being with the most gracious, most generous, most sophisticated of human beings. So far from being simple, they are very, very rich and complex'. Steeped in European languages from childhood, he was expected to acquire French, German and Hebrew. When in the Arctic, Brody learnt two Inuktitut dialects, and considers language to be the key to understanding other cultures. 'Language', he shares, 'reveals different ways of knowing our world. Hunter-gatherers around the world talk most intently about loss of language. To know the language is to have the stories about the place and have the detailed knowledge ... to lose it is to lose your own claim to the land ... to lose your links to the past and your links to the future'.

Brody has spent a long career devoted to telling the stories and advancing the rights of indigenous people. Since 1997, he has worked with the South African San Institute on oral history and land rights in the Southern Kalahari. He is an Associate of the Scott Polar Research Institute and was recently made Canada Research Chair in Aboriginal Studies at the University of the Fraser Valley.

PHOTOGRAPHY NOW

Let us first say what photography is not. A photograph is not a painting, a poem, a symphony, a dance. It is not just a pretty picture, not an exercise in contortionist techniques and sheer print quality. It is or should be a significant document, a penetrating statement, which can be described in a very simple term – selectivity.

BERENICE ABBOTT, 1951

The most difficult thing for me is a portrait. You have to try and put your camera between the skin of a person and his shirt. As time passes by and you look at portraits, the people come back to you like a silent echo. A photograph is a vestige of a face, a face in transit.

HENRI CARTIER-BRESSON, 1980

DISCUSSION

PHOTOGRAPHY NOW

HUW LEWIS-JONES WITH MARTIN HARTLEY

Martin Hartley: The first portrait I ever created was on an old plate camera. I was a student at art college. The sitter was a local plumber, a friend of my dad. We met in his cottage in a tiny hamlet in the Ashworth valley. His house was old-fashioned with stone framed windows that only let in tiny pools of light. I'd taken some artificial light with me, but didn't want to use it because I felt incapable of controlling the flashlight well enough then to create a natural mood. So I sat him by the tiny window and we chatted informally as I loaded the camera. Plate cameras have a way of seeing the world that is quite different from that of modern cameras. The time period between focussing the lens and then closing and releasing the shutter is almost sociable – taking seconds rather than fractions of a second. I urged him not to move while I prepared the camera.

The lens is then closed and the shutter cocked before setting the aperture on the lens. The 'film', which has been painted onto a glass plate, is gently loaded into the back of the camera and the dark slide removed before releasing the shutter to expose the film as a single frame. The dark slide is re-inserted back into the film holder to prevent the image from being re-exposed. The exposed plate is then removed, flipped round and reinserted, the shutter is wound, and the process of taking the image can be repeated. My early reverence for these old plate cameras enhanced my respect for polar photographers like Hurley and Ponting who went through this process for every frame they shot in their entire careers.

Huw Lewis-Jones: I know that you admire the work of these photographic pioneers, in particular. You read their books. We all enjoy their remarkable images. We are lucky enough to have over 1,700 original glass-plate negatives by Herbert Ponting in our collections at the Scott Polar Research Institute. We also look after some of this very early camera equipment: Ponting's Soho Reflex, Cherry-Garrard's old plate camera, and the Staley that Scott took with him to the Pole. These men have been an inspiration to many travel and exploration photographers. Can you recall the moment you decided to get out into the wilderness?

PREVIOUS PAGE: Travelling with dogs, offshore October Revolution Island, Severnaya Zemlya, February 2006

LEFT: Martin Hartley at 86 degrees on the frozen ocean, Adventure Ecology Trans Arctic Expedition, 2006.

MH: I was given my first camera when I was 5. It was boxed in an adventure kit along with an army-style water bottle, plastic binoculars, a compass and a gap where my mum had removed a penknife, so I wouldn't hurt myself. I spent hours pretending I was an explorer in the long 'tiger' grass in the fields behind our house. The first photographs I ever took on that camera, however, were not outdoor shots but black and white snaps of my sister and her friend skipping. At the age of 15 I embarked on my first 'expedition' – a 550-mile walk around the UK with two school friends during our summer holiday. I made a conscious decision to choose a small lightweight camera and took with me a Pentax 110 with interchangeable lenses. I naively chose the camera based on its aesthetics – I thought it was a beautiful object – and the hundreds of images I brought back were all disappointing because of the tiny negative it produced.

In 1993, I took a large format wooden plate camera with me on an expedition to the Himalayas. This experience gave me a brief insight into the amount of effort required to take a single photograph with an old camera in all but the most perfect weather conditions. Any amount of wind reduced the photographic possibilities dramatically. I returned from the expedition with only one photograph I was proud of. Simply being at the right place at the right time to 'get the shot' is not enough when shooting in inhospitable environments and poor weather conditions, both with early plate cameras and modern digital equipment.

HLJ: Among so many difficulties facing the photographer in the polar regions, the logistical challenge surely plays a major part?

MH: Yes, but it is important to distinguish between photographing a prolonged polar expedition and being on a relatively short 'adventure holiday', which is a completely different experience. Keeping photographic equipment working on an expedition takes some logistical juggling. You can't just plonk your camera on a radiator to thaw out at the end of the working day. On an expedition you constantly have to use your own body heat to keep the camera operational. The usual careful management of equipment – camera bodies, lenses, batteries, charging equipment, etc – is exacerbated ten-fold on an expedition, where any equipment failure might render the whole photographic process inert.

I once dropped a fully-charged spare battery in the snow on the Arctic Ocean whilst trying to replace a used one. Within seconds the contacts had gone green and

were fizzing. The cold slows down your reaction times and movement and makes clumsy mistakes more common. The cold will always find the weak point in any piece of equipment or person if there is one to be found. Advances in camera technology bring their own problems, with more reliance on batteries and sensitive electronics which don't cope well with the humidity and salty environment on the Arctic Ocean. Old plate cameras used by the likes of Hurley and Ponting would not have had these problems, but the lubricants used on shutters would have become viscous at lower temperatures, slowing the shutter movement and rendering it unreliable (which wouldn't have been noticeable until the processing stage). When I have shot 220 film below minus 30, the glue that holds the backing paper to the film loses its tack and often comes off completely in the back of the camera.

In 2009 I am due to photograph an expedition to the North Pole to measure the thickness of the polar ice. Assuming that there is no re-supply by plane, my photographic kit list, alone, might read like this:

- Two Nikon D3 digital cameras (one in re-supply)
- 25 x 8-Gigabyte flash cards (that's enough to shoot 75 frame shots a day for 4 months)
- One Nikon Speedlight 800
- 14–24mm zoom f2.8
- 24-85mm zoom f2.8
- 85mm f1.4 Prime lens
- 180mm f2.8 Prime lens
- Charging equipment yet to be decided
- Linhof Technorama 617-S III traditional film camera with f5.6/90mm lens, finder & centre filter
- 40 rolls of 220 Fuji Provis F 100 ASA film (that's enough for 320 frames)

Being a photographer in the polar environment demands that you have to endure the usual levels of discomfort with relative ease if you wish to free up some mental space for creative decisions above and beyond essential, instinctive decisions. The low temperatures compounded by limited time fuel a pressure that is unique to the environment.

Unless this formula is managed with competence, the extreme cold can have a rapid and increasingly serious impact on the physical and mental state of the photographer and his equipment. Ponting and Hurley clearly mastered this formula during their time on the ice. It is remarkable how Hurley found the mental energy to take photographs at all, let alone the beautiful images he shot.

LEFT: A selection of cameras from the SPRI collections, alongside those used by Martin Hartley. From top left: Kershaw Patent plate box camera belonging to Apsley Cherry-Garrard and used in Antarctica on the *Terra Nova* expedition, 1910-13; side and front aspect of the Kershaw 7 x 5 Soho Reflex camera belonging to Herbert Ponting and used in Antarctica on the *Terra Nova* expedition; A.E. Stanley camera used by Captain Scott at the South Pole in 1912; Sir Raymond Priestley's camera, *Terra Nova* expedition; Kodak Retina camera belonging to Leslie Quar and used in Antarctica during the Norwegian-British-Swedish Expedition, 1949-52; mobile phone used (rarely) by Martin Hartley; digital Nikon camera and Mamiya 645 Pro TL camera, with Seckor C 35mm lens, used by Martin Hartley, who has now completed 17 assignments to the polar regions.

HLJ: These early expedition photographers not only carried cameras and tripods but also large metal and wooden boxes containing glass bottles full of chemicals, developing tanks, paraffin heaters – even their own sink – and set up their own dark room on board ship or at base camp. Considering these limitations, it is incredible what men like Ponting were able to achieve. Modern photographers are now able to capture images that simply weren't possible with the equipment of the past.

MH: True, the lightweight super-mobile cameras and high-speed films of today allow the photographer to jump into a situation or scene that might explode in front of him. With no need for a tripod and the 'film' already in the camera, it is a relatively easy process to get into a position to grab a shot with minimal impact on the speed and direction of a moving expedition party. The ability to photograph an unguarded look or unplanned moment is the gift of modern camera technology.

There is a price to pay for this convenience. Batteries that power every part of the camera need re-charging and looking after. Holding onto a metal-bodied camera for long periods is a very good way to rapidly cool your fingers. The glue that holds backing paper onto medium format film stops sticking below the minus thirties. Tiny buttons on digital cameras need modification if they are to be accessed with big mitts on. This in itself adds a huge cost to an expedition

budget. Also, even though there are lighter cameras available, a full kit is still fairly cumbersome.

HLJ: Though in comparison it would seem expedition photographers today have a relatively easy time of it – neither having to build their own dark rooms, nor process their own film – new expectations and pressures have arisen. Most expedition photographers are expected to take both still photographs and film digital video and then send back the images using mobile satellite technology on the day of shooting. In 2004, using iridium phone technology, the young British athlete Ben Saunders sent back still and moving images from the North Pole.

MH: Yes, both the video and the still image were of surprisingly good quality and ideal for use on a website, but they required a huge amount of effort to send back, and they were not of a high enough quality for reproduction in print. I have been fortunate enough to be asked to film and photograph an expedition to the North Pole from Alaska in 2009 using revolutionary communications technology. The technology that has been developed for this expedition has been designed with two things in mind: to send back important ice data from the Arctic Ocean and, for the first time, both high resolution still and moving images, the intention being to narrow the gap between the experience of the 'explorer' and the viewer at home – a magic lantern slideshow for the modern age!

ABOVE: Herbert Ponting and his telephoto apparatus, January 1912.

Herbert Ponting at work in his darkroom, July 1911.

HLJ: That will be quite amazing. And yet, you have also enjoyed traipsing around Britain with me in the search for portraits?

MH: We have been welcomed into the homes of many of the explorers that we admire most. Though I've worked with many of the people I've photographed, I had never met some of the people before arriving to take their portrait for this project. Portraiture is an intimate act. The tone of the brief encounter between the photographer and subject affects the outcome of the image. The technical aspects of taking a photograph sometimes become insignificant. It is the dynamic of the human interaction between photographer and subject that directs the portrait.

The very act of embarking on a major polar expedition into one of the harshest environments on our planet is still a heroic one today, with high levels of risk and danger. Even with the development of reliable communication devices such as the Argos beacon or satellite telephone, re-supplies and rescue missions by air remain dependent on complex logistics and unpredictable weather and ice conditions. Nevertheless, the accessibility of both the Arctic and Antarctic by air and ship has allowed people with little polar knowledge and experience to reach both ends of the earth in relative safety and comfort. Whilst this has opened up the polar regions to a wider appeal, it has also contributed to a dense PR fog making it almost impossible for the general public and potential sponsors to know the difference between a fully guided tourist

and a genuine explorer in the classic sense of the word. We see images on websites and in newspapers of these self-branded often guided 'explorers' standing at the North and South Poles looking fresh-faced and wearing clothes without so much as a frayed seam, and their own PR media often fails to clarify the distance or time they have trekked.

HLJ: It was not our intention to compare, to make artificial hierarchies of achievement, but comparisons are inevitable. To photograph something in the first place is to confer importance, to accord value to someone, something, or an event. I also had little idea that curating an exhibition and creating a book like this was going to risk becoming such a political process. Over its year in the making, it was quite amazing the number of modern explorers/adventurers/ultimate-athletes/extreme-travellers who contacted me wanting to be in the book. A few were even willing to pay to feature in the selection.

MH: The modern polar world is competitive, and there are many people eager to attract sponsorship and support for their expeditions. Lots of people are desperate to try to give their trips that extra bit of credibility, or danger, to put them a step ahead of other travellers. I find it sad that people doing great things sometimes feel a need to overstate their achievements. Going to the North Pole is a huge achievement in itself, even if professional guides have been employed to break trail – it still requires

ABOVE: The ultimate 'extreme photographer', Frank Hurley would go to any lengths to get a good picture. Here he is wedged on the port yardarm high above the deck of *Endurance*, 'taking film from aloft', 1914.

Herbert Ponting with his 'photographic outfit on dog cart', with Master Johnson and Lassie, Christmas Eve 1911.

'The photographic dark room' of Herbert Ponting, 24 March 1911. Many of the objects shown here, including his camera and glass plate negatives, are now safely housed in the SPRI collections. Scott described the scene in his journal: 'Next is the dark-room in which Ponting spends the greater part of his life. Such a palatial chamber for the development of negatives and prints can only be justified by the quality of the work produced in it, and is only justified in our case by the possession of such an artist as Ponting. My eye took in the neat shelves with their array of cameras, etc, the lead-lined sink and automatic water tap, the two acetylene gas burners with their shading screens, and the general obviousness of all conveniences of the photographic art'.

ABOVE: Until the hut at Cape Evans was completed, much of the time was spent in a large green canvas tent. In this picture some of Scott's men are enjoying their lunch-break, 7 January 1911.

A Mountain Hardwear 'Space Station' 15-person 4-season expedition tent, Patriot Hills, November 2004.

'managing' your reputation. You'll be amazed though, bearing this in mind, how the discomforts, pressures and dangers of expeditions dominate and stopping to capture a photograph is always, without exception, underappreciated at the time. Photographers seem to be at the bottom of the food chain out in the field. Not helped by the fact that often the more dynamic and interesting photographs are taken at moments of high risk, such as when the rest of the team is putting up a tent in high winds or crossing thin ice on a wide lead.

I fight my natural instinct to be a team player and have missed two incredible photographs by putting down my camera and helping someone get out of a critical situation. At the beginning of an expedition, I now make a point of stating that when a typical expedition situation deteriorates into a state of pure survival, no matter how brief, my responsibility is primarily to document these rarely seen moments that are part of the very attraction of expedition life. Taking photographs in a potentially life-threatening situation could be viewed as uncaring at best, irresponsible at worst, but the photographer has to exercise his judgment at these times.

HLJ: Precisely, but you shouldn't be too critical of this relationship, between an explorer and the public. If one has to judge, then it is surely all about the expedition's actual achievements, the value of its scientific research for example, and not about the next 'dubious' first.

huge effort and is something to be genuinely proud of. Nothing needs to be hidden or overstated to achieve modern PR value.

HLJ: Of course, but this is nothing new. For many of the earliest explorers, even men like James Cook, presenting an attractive image of oneself and one's achievements was crucial in securing financial support and the backing of his peers, not to mention the support of family and friends. Captain John Ross, an Arctic explorer, mounted a number of panoramas and gave lectures in the 1830s, even a massive outdoor spectacle in London, to try to win the support of the public. Explorers like Shackleton and Peary gave hundreds of lectures to spread word of their achievements, and to have good photographs to wow your audience was absolutely vital.

MH: It often seems that for many people it is more important to secure a good photograph, than let achievements speak for themselves. I suppose it is about

MH: I grew up with the romantic notion that explorers were people who left the shores of their own country and ventured into an unknown to discover new things and bring knowledge back home for everyone to benefit from. I think the word 'explorer' has been abused to the extent that the media employ the word openly to describe anyone that is not going on a package holiday. The reason for this is perhaps our need for genuine and inspiring role models and our historic attachment to the great geographical explorers of our past. When Scott returned from the pole he died dragging 35lbs of geological specimens which carried information that led to the theory of plate tectonics. Amundsen, who beat Scott to the pole, raced there and back without documenting anything scientific. Both are 'explorers' in the romantic sense of the word but I prefer to reserve the word for marking achievements that have integrity. Of the modern day 'explorers' that I have had the privilege of meeting and working with, those who in my eyes have achieved more, tend to choose not to label themselves 'explorers' but succumb to the pressure of doing so, to compete with those who have achieved less and yet brand themselves readily with the accolade.

HLJ: Perhaps this reveals more than we might like to see; a glimpse of the modern face of exploration. Is it really all just sound bite, snapshot, priority squabbles and the best media story? Just as people are still contesting historic achievements, arguments still bubble over what makes an authentic 'first'; purists seem to be unanimous in their derision of tourists and wealthy adventuring as ruining the spirit of the 'game'. Some critics snipe that with GPS and satellite phones even solo expeditions can hardly claim to be unsupported. Many even call the whole pursuit a pointless and extravagant waste of money. This sort of scepticism is nothing new, yet most commentators now agree that expeditions need an end-game; to be imagined as valuable they need to be *relevant*. It is perhaps no longer enough just to challenge yourself.

Most now go North or South with the words 'education' or 'raising awareness' on their lips. And so, polar expeditions are cast as enlightening and philanthropic journeys, whilst also perhaps 'pioneering' in some new technique, or perhaps not. A few are arrogant enough to declare that they can 'make history'; one even suggested he could 'prove' it. Others are modest enough to hope that just a few people might be inspired by their struggles. Yet most explorers are eager to step forward as self-made ambassadors against the perils of global warming. So how exactly can polar exploration remain relevant? Scientific exploration, adding to the existing body of knowledge, certainly fits. Record-breaking does not. 'I'm not judging people' says Dan Bennett, President of the Explorers Club, treading carefully, 'but merely repeating another person's first and doing it faster or ... on a pogo stick ... that is athletics, not exploration'.

MH: It is interesting you should mention 'athletics' because, in fact, I think athletes have taken on the heroic role that used to be occupied by genuine explorers. We are fascinated by pushing our human boundaries and lose our respect rapidly when we learn that their performance has been dishonestly achieved (for example, drug enhanced). Unlike the sporting world, however, no credible organisation exists in the polar world to monitor and evaluate polar achievements. There is a great article written by a hero of mine, the

late Sir Wally Herbert, along with Richard Weber, Mikhail Malakhov and Sir Ranulph Fiennes, which sums this all up. It is called 'Earning the Applause' in which these polar veterans describe the really shameful and quite embarrassing way that some modern adventurers claim feats way beyond the facts, and certainly way beyond their talents.

Wally Herbert, however, was a true legend among polar explorers. He was not only a great writer and an artist, but he also travelled with dogs in the polar wilderness over 25,000 miles. He made maps of many unexplored regions of the Antarctic. His total time on the Arctic Ocean on one expedition was 477 days. Some modern 'explorers' on the lecture circuit these days have only gone on one expedition, maybe spending as little as 30 days on the ice, often with their hands held the whole time by a far more experienced guide. Yet, the guides often get no credit at all. These facts speak for themselves. All that many modern expeditions seem to prove is how difficult it must have been in the past, without our modern comforts and satellite communications for backup.

HLJ: Exploration has always been a drama of public presentation. Photographs are absolutely crucial, as much as a stunning painting, a detailed programme of laborious scientific measurements, or a well-written magazine article, in order to make an expedition's achievements known to as large an audience as possible. I guess this is even more acute in the polar regions, in the past in particular, as there is nothing to see at the height of an achievement. There is often no easy-to-see moment of completion like getting to the top a beautiful mountain; at the North Pole there

ABOVE: F.J. Hooper was persuaded by Ponting to pose for some publicity shots for the expedition's sponsors, in this instance fulfilling the obligation to Messrs. Heinz & Co, 9 January 1912.

A group of polar 'adventurers' pose during their Arctic expedition, sponsored by American Express, 2003.

ABOVE: Australian
cosmetic dental surgeon
Geoff Knight managed
just 1.5km of his epic
journey from Patriot
Hills to the South
Pole in 2003. 'I don't
understand', he said, 'it
worked bloody fine on
the beach in Melbourne!'

is little but white, a 'great geography of nothingness'. Unless of course there is a massive Russian ice-breaker nearby that day with a hold full of holidaymakers! Surely one of the big challenges is how to make a North Pole photograph attractive to a sponsor. How to make the polar prize look like something *worth* slogging all that way to?

MH: On the surface of it, yes, it does look like there is nothing there apart from absolutely 'nothing'. That is exactly the reason why people go there. Not to be stimulated by a myriad of distractions is a challenge in itself, as we are visually bombarded in our everyday lives. Photographically, the beauty of this is that it is relatively easy to give images strong visual gravity in this alien environment.

HLJ: Yet, geographically, because of this lack of an obvious, definite physical feature it is often the way achievements are reported, rather than the facts, on which expeditions are judged. Sadly, the most 'successful' are not always the most worthy of the public attention. And it is often how a polar trip is presented, that ensures it can grab headlines, and its leader can secure book deals or dates on the lecture circuit.

MH: I agree, and that's the sad thing because all too often the difficult things like science, pioneering journeys and honest hard work are forgotten in public stories in favour of dashes to the Pole, great rescues and

even greater failures. Photography plays its part in this, of course. Images are the powerful means to deliver exactly the kind of story that an individual wants to be told. However, often photographs upset this easy scenario, by telling the truth, and not the version of an adventure that the explorer, let-alone his audience, wants.

HLJ: What have you found is the 'type' of photograph that many of your explorer-clients want?

MH: That's easy. They want their own definitive, heroic shot. They want their struggles to be read across their faces. You can see it so clearly in the historic portraits too, and that's exactly what I get asked to reproduce. The stress of the emotional and physical separation from home and the absolute immersion into the polar environment for months at a time can be read in the faces of the early explorers; their iron will converted to an iconic image, cast in silver halide, 'the original thousand mile stare'. This is the sort of visual gravity that most modern-day explorers wish to see in their own portrait.

This iconography, more than any other image from an expedition, expresses human endurance and has become the hallmark. The image of a polar gladiator whose feeble and frayed armour has battled with the coldest cold, the strongest of unrelenting winds, and the stretching of starved sinew for many a remote, harsh month. This was the image that was taken home and became the explorer's marketing tool – and by association was both the reward and the lure for the sponsors, inspiring interest and fascination and encouraging funding for future expeditions. Even the original negatives themselves bear the tears and tales of polar travel and adventure.

HLJ: The stoic stare, the weather-beaten face, the frozen beard? It has become both a staple and something of a cliché. In 1909 even, a few days before he claimed to have reached the North Pole, the explorer Robert Peary scribbled in his notebook how he would like his public to see him when he got home: 'a portrait of me in a deer or sheep skin coat ... face unshaven ... a special print to bring out the grey eyes, the red sun burned skin, the frosted eyebrows, eyelashes and beard'. Are these still the key ingredients to make a marketable polar portrait?

MH: Definitely. Obviously, the extreme cold transforms our physical appearance but the 'frozen face' look is by far the most requested image from any polar shoot. Sometimes photographs are intended for a specific audience and I can't deny it, this sort of shot of frozen cliché really jumps up; it really takes you straight into the action, and it's an image to which almost anyone can easily relate.

I admit I have found it difficult *not* to take heroic portraits of many of the individuals selected for this book as my own respect for their extraordinary achievements has affected how I regard them. I have been lucky enough to have had the opportunity to meet so many of them out on the ice and to have been able to shoot them 'in action' in glamorous portraits. Though it is important to note, often I am taking these portraits not just for myself but also on assignment, working to a brief from a sponsor whose whole campaign is pitched at supporting adventurers as inspirational role models, pushing themselves to achieve extraordinary feats in the most challenging of circumstances.

The 'heroic' image is not just how I might see them but how they themselves want – and how the PR campaign behind them needs them – to be portrayed. The role of the modern polar expedition photographer is, for the most part, to document and capture inspirational images. Most modern explorers model their image on these early explorers and now, as then, many make their living by giving motivational talks to inspire others, recounting their adventures with images to support their stories.

HLJ: As well as being an admirer of explorers too, I confess to being a huge fan of the essays of the late Susan Sontag, activist, photographic historian and cultural theorist. She wrote beautifully, and perhaps more than anyone she has encouraged us to look *into* photographs, as well as simply looking at them. She was particularly interested in the way photographs have multiple uses. Images have careers; they are put to work. In the case of the exploration portrait the needs of a public profile and a profitable persona certainly direct the way a photograph is made.

The cultural historian James Ryan writes that 'photographs need to be understood not simply as visual repositories of some frozen history, but rather as complex moments in historical processes of representation'. Photographs are constantly re-employed to satisfy a range of uses and a range of audiences.

Photography is also an elegiac art, 'a twilight art' Susan Sontag suggests, in that photographs actively promote nostalgia. Photography also offers instant romanticism about the present. We are constantly scripting the way we want our present, as well as our pasts to be read. Photography is wrapped in sentimentality. Nostalgia can affect the way I might read an image, does it touch the way you take a photo?

MH: In some ways, yes. We cannot help but look with nostalgia at these old black and white portraits and allow our imaginations to question just what it was like to set off into the unknown, without hope of rescue or communication with the rest of the world. So we read their stories from their faces, trying to understand something of their thoughts and experiences. Modern day polar expeditions at least know what they are heading into and though the environment is as harsh and inhospitable and the dangers as ever present as they were for these early explorers, satellite communication means rescue is at least possible.

HLJ: The general introduction of colour was the major lasting innovation left of the twentieth century. It had been attempted from the very beginning, but the first practical colour film, Kodachrome, was only introduced in 1936 and, like television, it only really grew after the end on the Second World War. When the explorer Sir Vivian Fuchs published his account of his crossing of Antarctica in 1958, it came with a disclaimer to reassure its readers that the colours of their photographs were real and not a figment of the imagination. Some thought them too 'romantic'. George Lowe's marvellous photographs presented a continent of vivid colour. The public were used to seeing its polar heroes battle in black and white. Do clients ask you to shoot in monochrome, to lend a photograph a sense of history?

ABOVE: Shackleton's *Nimrod* expedition was the first ever to take a motor car to the Antarctic. Here Bernard Day, the expedition's electrician and mechanic, poses at the wheel of the 4-cylinder, 15-horsepower air cooled car from the Arrol-Johnston company. Shackleton was interviewed by the magazine *Autocar*, shortly before he left in 1907: 'He has provided himself with a real live motor car with which he hopes to reach his goal and hoist the Union Jack. Under favourable circumstances Lieutenant Shackleton computes that the machine can travel 150 miles in twenty four hours and … he thinks there would be a fair chance of sprinting to the pole'.

ABOVE: One of Britain's finest polar explorers, the late Sir Wally Herbert, photographed at his home in the Scottish Highlands, 2006.

MH: Clients tend to leave me to it to decide. It is actually quite hard to get black and white images printed in magazines nowadays, so clients tend to prefer colour. Since the advent of colour I think that black and white photographs are generally perceived as being closer to art as they are further away from reality, simply by being black and white. It's also tempting to brand a black and white image as nostalgic. Again with modern digital technology it is possible to obtain relatively good-looking black and white images from a colour original. Not ideal, of course, but it does add flexibility if it's not possible to carry two types of film or carry cameras with interchangeable film backs. In an ideal world, if the intention was for the image to be shot in black and white then it should be shot on black and white at the point of capture, otherwise the image is in danger of losing some of its original integrity.

Instinctively, I tend to shoot landscape format portraits, contextualising the subjects in their environment and this has been an interesting point of discussion in the process of editing for the book. Portraiture has changed since these historic portraits were taken and so too has exploration. Some of my favourite portraits have not been included here. As you know, it was so hard just to choose 50.

HLJ: But that is why photography, as much as being a record of a moment, is an art form. As an art, people are free to make up their own mind about what they like, or what they don't like. The only certain thing is that it is often very hard to have exactly the same choices. This book could be described as an album of quotations. Selection has to play a part, but some of your great photographs, such as your portraits of Ran Fiennes and Wally Herbert, are quite brilliant no matter the manner in which they are presented.

MH: It is hard often to get enough distance to see the good and the bad things about a particular portrait and often you have to content yourself knowing that a picture you don't like might be exactly the shot a client wants, and vice versa. There are also loads of photographs that we both would have liked to have taken, but explorers are hard people to track down, and we just didn't have enough time to arrange the sittings. It was hard too to justify the carbon footprint required to go and reach many of these people.

HLJ: Of course, there are many famous explorers, scientists and polar travellers not included here, and certainly many hundreds of people whose achievements deserve a place in this mix.

MH: There are a number of people that I would have loved to include, Erling Kagge, Rune Kelder, Park Young. I know we were both saddened by the recent death of Dr Roy 'Fritz' Koerner, a man whose achievements as an explorer and glaciologist are unmatched, certainly in the modern day. I was also lucky enough to be able to meet the great Sir Wally Herbert shortly before he died – a man who was a longstanding friend of Fritz, whom he led on their crossing of the Arctic Ocean – and to enjoy many of their stories.

HLJ: Both were great men, and that portrait of Wally in particular is a special one. There is real fire in his eyes; the shot speaks volumes about his drive and ability as one of our greatest explorers, whilst also being a compassionate man and a remarkable artist. Few men, let alone explorers, have such rounded talents. This is one of your favourite portraits, isn't it? You also took a number of black and white portraits that day in Scotland.

MH: I travelled up to Scotland with my large format plate camera and enough black and white sheet film to sink a battleship. I chose a plate camera and black and white film as I wanted to cast Wally back into that great generation of true explorers – people who had risked a lot, people who had created footsteps where no man had been before, people who had brought more back than a mere record. To my huge disappointment I discovered when I got there that the glass in the back of my plate camera had shattered in transit. Fortunately I had my trusty medium format Mamiya camera with me as a back-up. The end result was exactly what I had been looking to achieve, though if I'm honest, not being able to shoot his portrait on a plate camera meant something was missing from the negative.

HLJ: Martin, more than many people, you have come face to face with some of the most famous explorers of our generation. Do you have any other obvious favourites?

MH: I think Ran Fiennes is often underestimated – so much has been learnt from his early expeditions, often taken for granted by people following in his footsteps. It was seeing the footage of him being picked up after his Trans-Antarctic expedition that really sparked off my interest in the polar regions. Surprisingly, Ran is not entirely comfortable with the label 'explorer', such is his respect for the men that have gone before him. He is a huge character and great to be around.

I have been on assignment to the polar regions 17 times and have taken part in one Trans-Arctic expedition so have the utmost respect for the Arctic Ocean, but

ABOVE: One of Britain's leading polar athletes, Rosie Stancer, on the eve of her departure for the North Pole, 2007.

I have never been brave enough to undertake a solo expedition. I shot this portrait of Rosie Stancer the evening before she set off on her Mars North Pole Solo expedition in February 2007. I spent the last 10 days with Rosie before she set off. I've been privileged to spend time with several North Pole soloists, and there comes a point on the eve of departure where the energy of preparation dissipates and is replaced by stillness and reflection. It happens every time. This image captures that moment and is heavy with contemplation. It's not about beautiful light but about a very private moment and internal stillness. This is the photographic eye of the storm of a North Pole Solo expedition. The next day Rosie departed from Ward Hunt Island on her bid to become the first British woman to reach the North Pole solo.

HLJ: Like you say, there is something incredibly powerful in her stillness here. As one might expect, there is a sense of nervousness, apprehension, yet also a sort of calm. This is calm that comes from her experience and skill. We can see her confidence in knowing that preparations are in place, and sense her excitement to get out on the ice.

MH: Yes, this stillness is something that we don't see a lot of in the historic images of explorers. What we rarely see published are the mundane, unglamorous moments of total boredom, stress and the chronic fatigue that are a bigger part of expedition life than those gigantic heroic moments, the posed moments that are celebrated, sometimes too often. The moments of stillness and waiting are agonising but also fascinating to me. The days spent waiting for the weather to turn, the multiple hours or days of sitting in a small tent with no food, waiting for a re-supply to arrive. The packing, unpacking and re-packing of equipment. There is really nothing glamorous about a North Pole expedition.

We are lucky to be able to publish many rare historic images in this book, exactly the kind of behind-the-scenes images that are so interesting to me, yet were never originally published in books or lectures about these old expeditions. There are, of course, reasons why many more photographs like this were not captured. The expensive and bulky film would have been saved for precious moments or staged shots, and the time taken to set up a tripod and focus a lens before clicking the shutter would have been too long a period to capture a fleeting moment. These sorts of rapid, spontaneous shots are now made possible by advances in camera technology.

HLJ: Those are certainly some of the best shots, aren't they? So often beautiful, hilarious, vulnerable, intriguing, they can give us genuine insights into what life must be like. The challenge now, I suppose, is to try to stage the spontaneous. To try and grab that fleeting moment, whilst the subject also realises that's the kind of shot that is wanted too.

MH: It's hard to document all the pre-expedition preparations because there is just so much non-photographic work to be done. Unless you want to be perceived as a 'deadweight' you have to get stuck in with the jobs to hand. Trying to emulate expedition life when not on an expedition is also hard. Trying to find appropriate locations to create 'expedition reality' is half of the job. Without realistic terrain, it's not always possible to create the correct *action*. For example, when I was photographing Ben Saunders in Khatanga in 2004 before his attempted Arctic Ocean traverse from Russia, there were no pressure ridges because we were inland. The best place to shoot Ben 'going over a pressure ridge' was the local snow covered tip! Not hugely glamorous but effective in making the scene look completely right.

I particularly love this portrait of a woman at the weather station in Sredni. The most northerly habitation in Siberia, the station is manned by two husband and wife teams who work continuously for two years then break for six months before the next two-year shift. Polar bears are a constant threat. Yet the biggest challenge they face, on a daily basis, is boredom. Individuals like these don't chase heroic images of themselves though they endure sub-zero conditions for months on end and enjoy few frills or comforts. Interestingly, the fact that both couples have been living up at Golomyanniy for twenty years says a lot about how much they enjoy what they do for a living.

HLJ: The American photographer Lewis Hine joked, 'If I could tell the story in words, I wouldn't need to lug a camera'. There is, of course, something special to photography, its ability to show the world and its peoples in ways often impossible to convey in words, certainly difficult unless you are a master travel writer like Wilfred Thesiger, Eric Newby, or even Apsley Cherry-Garrard.

MH: It was Cherry who famously described polar exploration as 'at once the cleanest and most isolated way of having a bad time which has been devised'. Mind you, he wasn't a bad photographer either. Certainly, some

RIGHT: A selection of behind-the-scenes portraits from the modern polar world. From top left: Inuk employee of the Resolute Bay power corporation, March 2003; British adventurers Simon Murray and Pen Hadow with kit in their hotel room in Punta Arenas, November 2003; the tea-lady and scientific observer Svetlana Omelchenko at the Golomyanniy Meteorological Station, Severnaya Zemlya, March 2006; David de Rothschild in his tent at 85 degrees on way south from the North Pole towards Ward Hunt after 92 days on the Arctic Ocean, June 2006; and Dr Victor Boyarsky, at 86 degrees on the Russian side of the Arctic Ocean in a M16 helicopter, March 2006.

ABOVE: The polar portrait in modern media, *Geographical* magazine, 2005.

MH: Everything interests me photographically – people, landscapes, sport, beauty. I'm currently working on a personal project about fatigue and how it manifests itself physically in the body and more interestingly perhaps, in the face. Whether it's a surgeon who's just spent fourteen hours piecing someone's hand back together or an Olympic rower who has just finished a training session, there is a fleeting moment when their state of mental exhaustion appears on their face as a kind of despair. It's this moment that I am interested in capturing; a state of being that is impossible to replicate even by the greatest of actors.

Perhaps this interest was born out of reading stories of polar suffering. You can clearly see what I am talking about in the face of every single person standing at the South Pole on 18 January 1912. I recently returned from a shoot in the jungle in Vietnam where one of the people we were with became hyperthermic. His condition was manifested in the stress in his whole physique and in particular in his face.

Yet I am also still drawn to the polar regions, particularly the Arctic Ocean. Unlike the unique view from the top of mountains, there is nothing at the North Pole. It is even hard to know when you are on it apart from the GPS reading indicating 90 degrees. Photographs become proof of the event and as such carry weight, power and responsibility. The responsibility of the photographer on an expedition overtook that of the expedition artist. Photographs became the cast iron documents of the truth of exploration, a physical proof of places visited and of peoples discovered. Huge importance was placed on photography in the polar regions, as a by product of cutting-edge exploration. The camera became the most important of expedition tools that was to document the greatest acts of human endeavour, discovery and heroism to be found outside a war zone.

Hurley walked off the ship when Shackleton demanded full copyright of his images and it was Hurley who saved the plates when *Endurance* sank – as these were the first images from this remote end of the world. Hurley, more than Shackleton, realised that if nobody survived, the photographs would tell the world the story of the expedition. Though we know Hurley doctored his plates, long before sophisticated computer programmes made it possible for vast image manipulation, so how truthful a document the photograph is remains questionable.

pictures are worth a thousand words. They offer instant stories. They let you share in a moment immediately. The stories and images these early explorers brought back with them continue to inspire people to follow in their footsteps and seek adventure. The North and South Geographic Poles remain the ultimate test of human physical and mental endurance. I try to offer a glimpse of these challenges in the photographs I bring back.

HLJ: Many of your photographs are for clients, for advertising, or for the necessary self-promotion of an explorer making a career. But what about photos taken for the sheer pleasure of it all, what about the ones you want to take?

HLJ: Photography's supremacy as the tool for representing fact was well summed up in Emile Zola's famous declaration – 'We cannot claim to have really seen anything before having photographed it'. Yet, the idea of truth in photography is problematic. Photographs show and at the same time reveal very little. Barthes' influential essay on photography, *Camera Lucida*, argued for the recognition of the objective powers of the photograph – its capacity to fix a moment, offering the viewer some degree of certainty – yet the ambivalence of photography surely is its ability to jump beyond this sort of function. The other difficulty is that there are always changes in the way photographs are viewed; each person brings different ideas of image, memory and, perhaps, competing inspirations to translate and decode a photograph.

MH: I always try to take honest photographs, and by that I mean photographs that accurately represent the scene witnessed and photographed: photographs that don't create unnecessary illusions. It's tempting as a photographer to try and make situations look more than they are. I am very lucky in that the reality I am often confronted with is enough to make a picture interesting. At its simplest, I'm trying to show places and people, and part of the real beauty of photography is that it can transport us to places that are difficult to imagine.

HLJ: In photography's early decades, photographs were expected to be perfect images. This is still the aim of most amateur photographers, for whom the perfect picture is something beautiful to look at; a smiling face, an attractive woman, or a setting sun dipping below the horizon. Photographs are selective, they are idealised.

Yet the earliest portrait photographs, mostly the daguerreotype, insisted upon their realism. They were 'truths of nature, gifted by the sun'. They were literally mirror images of those photographed. It became a means of reporting, a tool of truth. And still the portrait photograph declares itself as the *trace* of the person, before the eye. The photograph validates identity – be it on a driving licence, an official form, or a passport – and it has the status of an authentic signature of the person sitting before the camera. Yet we know, of course, that the portrait can tell us as much about the photographer, or the aspirations of its subject. The authority of the photographic image is often unquestioned, but we know that, far from being objective and neutral, photographs are highly selective.

Looking at the portrait of an individual is to invite all sorts of speculations as to who they were, or are, what they might have thought, how they might act. Portraits encourage us to ask questions. The late Ansel Adams remarked that 'there are always two people in every picture: the photographer and the viewer'. How do you think people respond to your portraits?

MH: I don't see myself as a portrait photographer, but I do love taking photographs of people. When I take a portrait my main objective is to make the person look as good as they can, often because I have had a good experience meeting them. I'm aware this could be viewed as a bit shallow in the world of portrait photography, but I like to think my photographs reflect the integrity of the people I photograph. A friend of mine told me 'if you can't find anything good to say about someone, then don't say anything'. Perhaps I have adopted this view in my portrait photography, why would I want to photograph someone I don't like, when I could be photographing someone I do?

I always try to take honest photographs … It's bloody tempting as a photographer to try and make situations look more than they are.

What is clear is that people bring lots of different things to a picture when they look at it; an idea of history, or someone's reputation. Because of this, people take different things away from a picture, often way beyond what I might have hoped for or imagined for the photograph in the first place. That is why photography is an *art* – people are free to interpret it and make up their own minds about the quality or message of a particular shot, not to mention how they might feel interested, or not, by its subject.

Scott and Shackleton took professional photographers on their expeditions because they recognised the value of excellent photographs not only to document their expedition but also to sell their stories. I think Herbert Ponting was really the first to bring an artistic eye to the science of photographing polar expeditions. In Scott he found a leader willing to give him the opportunity to pursue his art in the most technically challenging and artistically inspiring part of the world he would ever

ABOVE: British
adventurer Pen Hadow,
with kit, on frozen
Resolute Bay, 2003.

encounter. After Ponting came Hurley, of course, who went on to chronicle Shackleton's 1914-17 Imperial Trans-Antarctic Expedition, which became well documented and certainly the greatest polar rescue mission ever. It's not unusual, on any expedition, for the photographer to be perceived as surplus to requirements. The value of the professional photographer only becomes apparent when images of the expedition appear in print.

With advances in technology and most people owning cameras and having experience of taking photographs themselves, many modern expeditions opt to shoot their own images and not bother with a trained photographer at all. The digital revolution demands us to raise the bar for quality as professionals, whilst it makes it easier for everyone to 'be a photographer'.

HLJ: Yes, the technological aspects of photography mark major cultural moments. The invention of the dry plate camera, in the 1870s was a development as significant as the current shift from film-based to digital photography – dry plate marked photography's passage from a large handcrafted industry to a mechanised, industrial process. This was the beginning of mass production. It

made it possible for the general public to become photographers as well as consumers of photography. Photography's success was also dependent as much on technological innovation, as the way it was circulated – spread about in books, magazines, postcards, and in advertising.

It all began with George Eastman. From 1879 to 1900 his company, Kodak of Rochester, New York, transformed photography with a series of inventions that took the medium from professional photographers to the man and woman in the street. This was a hand-held box camera loaded with enough film for a hundred exposures. Once finished you would send it off and later small prints arrived, together with the camera reloaded with another film. 'You Press the Button, We Do the Rest' was the company's famous slogan. This was the beginning of a snapshot culture, the birth of the *habit* of being photographed.

MH: And the trend in the twentieth century was to make photography quicker, easier, and less expensive for everyone. The film format of choice was 35mm, though there were attempts to introduce other formats. Most of these didn't last long, I suppose just like many of the inventions in photography's early days in the middle of the nineteenth century.

Technology has moved so quickly since then. I now spend most of my time now processing my images on a computer. Cameras are getting smaller and smaller, and technologies are incredibly sophisticated. You can choose to do without film altogether. Cameras employ sensors to record the image as digitally encoded information, which is stored and edited on a computer, printed, and shared across the globe at the click of a mouse. This is the biggest technical advance since dry plate.

HLJ: We are photographed almost everywhere we go, driving in our cars, shopping, existing. The digital revolution has transformed the art of the photograph. But does it mark the beginning of the end for film? Does it transfer complete control to anyone who can master electronic image manipulation software? What are we losing, indeed, what have we already lost?

MH: It is a very interesting point, and one often talked about when photographers get together. First of all I will say this – I love film and I also love digital technology. Both have a rightful place in the photographer's toolbox. Film photography will be around for as long as there are film cameras to put film into. Digital photography has made the technical aspects a lot easier for the user. What the advances in technology have not improved is a photographer's way of seeing. This is an indefinable and wholly organic process and not something currently available on a floppy disc, CD, DVD or even a blue ray thing. Artificial intelligence has a lot of catching up to do in this department.

In the polar regions it is now fairly straightforward to take a photograph, but that doesn't mean it will be a good one. It is also quite straightforward to pass these photographs back home. BAS bases have almost 24-hour Internet. As a tourist you may email from your cabin on a polar cruise ship, whilst sipping a cappuccino from a heavy porcelain mug.

We live in a world saturated with images, and newspapers are not always discerning; happy to publish images of any quality, even those taken on mobile phones, if newsworthy. Any image is better than no image. It is now common for expedition images to be sent back by satellite phones to blogs, web pages and newspapers. There is interest in the idea of seeing an image taken only today or yesterday in a remote part of the world and sent back by technology for all to see it – the *immediacy* of it is inspiring in itself, and brings the adventure closer to home.

ABOVE: Martin Hartley secures the shot, with ladder, on frozen Resolute Bay, 2003.

ABOVE: Modern recreation of Captain Lawrence Oates' final struggle, based on the famous painting 'A Very Gallant Gentleman' by J.C. Dollman. Waking on the morning of 17 March 1912, and recognising the need to sacrifice himself in order to give his companions a chance of survival, Scott wrote that Oates said to them 'I am just going outside and may be some time'. Oates left the tent, walking to his death into the teeth of a blizzard. His body was never found.

RIGHT: Some polar adventurers rest during their Arctic expedition, sponsored by American Express, 2003. Their journey traced the possible route taken by survivors of Sir John Franklin's expedition, from Victoria Island to Starvation Cove, just North of Boothia Peninsula. On the right of the picture is Ralph Baker Cresswell, a descendant of one of the original expedition members, and on the left is the BBC cameraman employed to capture their heroics on film.

HLJ: Timing is a key point – we want to see action as it happens. So quality is sacrificed for immediacy. But the real achievement with polar photography, like other really remote or hostile areas, is actually going there all the way and coming back. But photography also enables our ideas to travel far beyond ourselves. People are sending images to each other as never before – photography, after all, is about communication. You can share photos from your mobile phone standing on the bus, sitting in a coffee shop, or smiling proudly from the top of a mountain. The possibilities are endless. Online, anyone can publish their photographs to an almost limitless audience.

MH: It is incredible that, thanks to the digital age we are living in, sending images from a polar region back home is now possible within minutes. To watch digital video footage that is just a few hours old on a computer screen or television, of 'explorers' fighting their way across a surface that is now melting because of global warming is very powerful. I would suggest that this is one of the best uses of digital technology and one that Hurley, Ponting and Scott and Shackleton would all have wished they had had.

HLJ: This new age actually shares so much with the 'then', a world in which the brave photographer laboured in a cloud of chemicals in the darkroom, or huddled inside an exposing tent. Though all you now require is a computer, camera and printer, you also need a considerable amount of skill. There is still something quite Victorian about it, I suppose. Photography has returned to its 'do-it-yourself' roots. We can control our own taking, developing, enhancing and sharing. Though the camera has travelled a long way from its earliest days, the photography of now is not so far from the photography of the past. In portraits old and new the faces are much the same, it's just what our eyes have seen that is so vastly different. We are all still driven by a shared impulse: to imagine, to want to explore the world and to record our place within it.

London, 2008

THE BOUNDARIES OF LIGHT

> To take a photograph is to participate in another person's mortality, vulnerability, mutability. Precisely by slicing out this moment and freezing it, all photographers testify to time's relentless melt.
>
> **SUSAN SONTAG,** *ON PHOTOGRAPHY,* **1977**

AFTERWORD

THE BOUNDARIES OF LIGHT

HUGH BRODY

Polar travellers seem to make the most extreme and alarming kind of journey. They appear to travel from what is at the core of being human, the hearth and home and gentleness and certainties of everyday life, to a core of what is beyond the human, the cold and storm and ultimate homelessness of that which would seem to be uninhabitable. At the frontier between the possible and impossible, the regions of warm home and cold homelessness, there is a transition from safe into unsafe, tamed into wildness, culture into nature. The excitement and challenges of this frontier have many dimensions, make many appeals - to the imagination, to a sense of adventure and to some of the structures of human society and life. Little wonder, then, that images of the frontier can often have extraordinary power.

Standing at an edge, aware of taking steps out of what we know into what we don't know, or from safety into danger, there can be a powerful impulse to make a record of the moment. And there are two directions in which to look, two kinds of impression to record. Turn backwards, face those who say farewell and see the landscapes of home becoming a last glimpse of safety. There, as we leave them, are images we want to take with us: the snapshot of loved ones in a wallet or images that we might be able to pull out and share with our fellow adventurers or maybe with the tribal peoples we are expecting to encounter. These snapshots of ourselves and of memory may be comforting and also a substitute for words. With them we can know who we most like to think we are, and show others that we have lives that are not restricted to how we seem. Images that suggest that

PREVIOUS PAGE: A group of Greenlandic Inuit at Angmagssalik, a remarkable unpublished portrait taken by F.S. Chapman on the British Arctic Air Route Expedition, 1930-31.

LEFT: Ben Saunders, testing his equipment on a rubbish dump in Khatanga, 2004.

we are not really alone, adventuring and somehow lost: our beloved holding our baby, the mother ship from which we launch the kayak and the dogteam. Images to offer – to ourselves and to others – some warming, encouraging reassurance.

Then we turn and face the other way, our backs to home, our faces into the wind and the cold, and set off in our different degrees of solitude, into whatever levels of lostness and danger we are entering, embracing. The self as the vulnerable and defiant. As we move beyond the boundary, into the frontier, we take a different kind of photograph. We see one another, and have ourselves pictured, as explorers. We are constructed and equipped, inside and out, to do some kind of battle. The photographs are of the outside equipment but evoke the internal endeavour. These images at the outset will turn out to be openers of a series: the journey goes into wilder and more extreme places, misadventure adds to adventure, things are lost, found, the land is crossed, scaled, discovered for what it is or, more often, for the extremes that it can be. This is about coldness, emptiness, struggle, and many kinds of heroic undertaking in a defiance of nature that takes place as deep within the natural world as we can go.

When explorers pose for their own photographs, the presentation of the adventure has its own complications, its own self-consciousness. A wish to convey strength and determination, to offer a glimpse of adventure; or a wish to do the opposite, and offer a message that is somehow domestic and ordinary despite, and in contrast or opposition to, the wildness of the place and

unspoken reality of the wild. We look back at the camera, and through the camera to our friends and loved ones, smiling with pleasure at sharing this spot, this frontier. A flash of light from far away on the edge that will reach to others, to the future, to home.

The portrait Scott and his team took of themselves at the South Pole is an icon at an extreme: the end of the journey that has suffered great hardship and disappointment, and is going to suffer yet more. The best known portrait of Knud Rasmussen, taken in the early stages of the Fifth Thule Expedition, is an image that evokes a different, more gentle or reflective kind of undertaking. Then there are the wonderful photographs taken in the 1950s in the Canadian central Arctic by Richard Harrington, in which the complications of Inuit life are registered with such delicate poignancy. In each of these cases, the camera is pointed in a different kind of direction, to express a different kind of reality. Different enough to suggest caution when it comes to generalisations about what polar photography is and is not.

In the early days of photography, the two kinds of images, at and beyond the boundaries of culture and nature, home and exploration, were more self-conscious, dependent on technology that was cumbersome and in need of set-up. The subjects must be arranged, must hold still in front of the photographer. They must pose in a landscape that itself becomes a kind of photographer's studio. As cameras get smaller, simpler, more reliable and cheaper, with shutter speeds faster and f-stops options wider and then automated, the images need not be so

ABOVE: Some of the fascinating unpublished photographs in the SPRI collections, taken at Angmagssalik and on the shores of Sermilik Sound during the British Arctic Air Route Expedition, 1930-31.

RIGHT: Children of Gjoa Haven at the Hamlet Day celebrations, 2003.

posed. Life can be caught in action, but also life can be photographed dozens of times, from all angles. So the accumulation of images is so great that the selection of the good image becomes the creative task far more than the making of any one of them.

Thus it is in this project. In finding, choosing and ordering a collection of images, Huw Lewis-Jones has the most challenging task of all. He makes this work by editing a display from archives, making sense from proliferation. The challenge of this is both intellectual and creative: the creation of the exhibition and this book is to make us see and think, to offer images for our gaze but also to redirect that gaze. To make this book is to take a journey into the history of photography, into the meaning of a set of images, as also into the lives and, to some extent, the minds of those who are portrayed. This is a profound and large task, superbly executed, leaving us with the challenge of the images as well as the great pleasure of having them collected and curated.

In the era of light and sophisticated cameras, the images of far North and South are abundant. For all the ease and proliferation of the image-making, this shift is from less to more intimate, and so gives a sense of finding that the exploration of cold places may, after all, include moments that are not altogether dramatic and tough and lit by a triumph over hardship. Polar photography came to be the business of photographers rather than explorers themselves – though some of these photographers, not least the remarkable Martin Hartley, have to travel alongside explorers to get their images. Often, photographers spend a lot of time getting to know where they are, and the people they meet.

ABOVE: 'Captain Scott in his den', 7 October 1911. Scott spent much of his time at Cape Evans making entries in his journals and writing letters. On his bed is his beloved uniform overcoat, 'spared neither rain, wind, nor salt sea spray, tropic heat nor Arctic cold', and pinned on the wall are photos of his loved ones. 'The photography craze is in full swing', he wrote the previous evening, 'Ponting's mastery is ever more impressive, and his pupils improve day by day; nearly all of us have produced good negatives'.

Many, if not most, of the photographers who travel to the North have found themselves taking pictures of the people who live there. This can create an intriguing balance, and is the paradox I referred to: an inevitable appeal of the polar regions is the extremity of climate, the snow and ice, the hoar frost on the explorer's face, as well as the endless expanses of white and treeless wilderness. As Ranulph Fiennes says in his foreword to this book, journeys in these lands can mean 'a challenge just to stay alive'. Those at home who will enjoy the images (and buy the books and fund the next expedition) want the coldness, need the sense of the extreme, the battle between man and nature that is embedded in ideas about and much of the practice of polar travel. Yet the image that reveals and celebrates the extremes of cold and hardship is somewhat at odds, of course, with the realities of those peoples for whom the North is home.

Many of the early images of these peoples are of guides and hosts, men and women whom explorers depended on to make an exploration. The paradox of this is pervasive in the history of great and daring journeys. The European heroics in the harshest landscapes are played out on the safe side of disaster (for the most part) because of the help the Europeans get from people for whom these landscapes are some part of their backyard. In the photographs of Robert Flaherty, whose remarkable still images are less well known than his film *Nanook of the North*, the people of the Arctic are portrayed as smiling, innocent and triumphant. For Flaherty, the Inuit exemplify how the human spirit is made rich and happy by its being pitted against a fierce and cruel natural world. In this way, Flaherty's work is of a piece with what might be called 'explorer heroics'. He is determined that the Inuit in *Nanook* (just like the Irish peasantry in his other masterpiece, *Man of Arran*) be heroes of humanity, triumphing over dreadful odds. This is a concept of the people in relation to geography that is like many popular ideas of the explorer. In both cases, the achievement is through struggle against nature.

Since Flaherty, the message has shifted: as anthropology came to invite a much more careful and respectful view of peoples of all environments, so photographers from the south began to represent northern peoples as just as at ease with their landscapes and weather as any other peoples. Perhaps this is to understate or elide the importance to all northern travellers of the extremes – the beauty and the light of the Arctic are so linked to geography and weather as to mean few photographers would turn their lenses away from them. But the intimate black and white photography of Ulli Steltzer in the 1970s, for example, or much of the northern work of Bryan and Cherry Alexander across the last 30 years, along with the immersion in Inuit life of photographers like Robert Semeniuk and Paul Nicklen, all testify to a commitment to make images in the North that suggest that here is a land where, in truth, it is quite possible to live. They take us to culture far more than to nature.

This is not so, of course, in the Antarctic where no indigenous populations ever lived. Here the explorers struggle without the help of those for whom the wilderness is home; and they are all the more heroic for it, and their hardships are the more extreme, their achievements the more sure, for being all their own making. The images of Antarctic exploration are therefore far more crafted in heroics and extremes than is the case with Arctic photographers and their modern images. Even the most recent portraits of Emperor Penguins take special delight in the seemingly intolerable conditions in which the males incubate the eggs, huddled together against the freezing violence of the weather. Such images cause us to shudder in sympathy and amazement and to feel an awe for those who would dare to venture into such a place.

These flashes of light are a curious, fascinating mixture of truth and fiction. The truth is that of all still photography: here is an indisputable flicker of reality. The fiction is in the message, intended or unconscious, about what this reality is. Explorers do not always spend their time in a grim battle for survival; it might be said that the most successful journey was one in which no such battle ever had to be joined. Yet some do: journeys go wrong and some are designed to be as hard as possible. Yet the

construction of exploration as the stoic and heroic struggle is to some extent required: they satisfy the desire in the south that these journeys be hard fought, hard won, or magnificent in failure.

As we look at the portraits of those who are celebrated for their polar journeys, we might wonder what truths are held in these flashes of light in the camera, and what representations are being made from the look in the eye, the turn of the head, the choice of clothing, the moment that is being preserved, the photograph that an author or editor or publicist might choose for the cover of a book. The moment chosen is a choice about a version, and perhaps a subversion, of truth.

I rarely took photographs when in the North. Not because of any thoughts about versions and subversions of truth. I think I would have been only too happy to have my rather undangerous journeys made to seem at least a little heroic. The reason lay elsewhere: somehow to carry a camera caused me to look for pictures rather than look at the place itself. I would find myself framing pieces of the world to make an image, to set up some message, to capture and convey fragments of what was around me rather than just be there, letting the place take its own course. To look for the photograph seemed to be to fail to see, or to fail to be, without reference to how this might appear to others. I suppose some element of this was the temptation to show the exotic, to find the appearance of reality that would surprise or delight others, with a concomitant framing-out of that which might get in the way of the surprise, might diminish the exotic or indeed the achievement of being there. So I did not carry a camera, and only began to make images of the North when working on films – an altogether different form of photography.

When spending time in Sanikiluaq, in 1973, an Inuit community on the Belcher Islands off the coast of Arctic Quebec, my friends there gave me a camera as a birthday present. It was a quite basic camera that could be bought at the Hudson's Bay Company store on the islands. One of those who made the gift said that they had noticed I did not have a camera with me, and they thought I should be taking pictures to look at when back at home. I was moved and delighted but unsure what to do. I had a sudden idea: why don't you take the pictures, I said. You can choose what you think I should have, the photo mementos I should take away with me. So the camera was taken back and over the coming week or so some rolls of film were taken for me by my Inuit friends.

ABOVE: Photographs from Hugh Brody's personal collection, taken by his Inuit companions during a stay in Sanikiluaq, Arctic Quebec in 1973.

These photographs are remarkable for being domestic and personal. All the images are of people I spent most of my time with in my cabin or their homes or, in one series, at a community dance. No shots of the landscape or of hunting trips; nothing to show the climate or environment, except as very incidental backgrounds. There is not a flash of heroism, not a glimmer of any claim that anyone is doing anything other than going about their everyday life. One beautiful image is of an elder doing a string game: he

I had a sudden idea: why don't you take the pictures, I said. You can choose what you think I should have, the photo mementos I should take away with me.

was a man who had spent much time trying to teach these games to me and the photographer wanted me to have a record of his efforts. Another is of a young man turning with some skill and elegance in a square dance, again, a reminder to me: people used to joke about his particular enthusiasm for these dances. No ice floes and no storms and certainly no pictures from the few times we got into difficulties on hunting trips: no one would pause in the middle of the problems to take a photograph; solving the problem rather than any wish to record it occupied everyone's attention.

The photographs of Peter Pitseolak represent the most extensive and sustained making of Arctic images that come from within the North. Pitseolak, who was born and lived his life in the Cape Dorset area, met Robert Flaherty in 1912 when he was shooting his first footage for *Nanook of the North*. This encounter gave Pitseolak a sense of what photography could achieve, and also that it could all be done in the North – Flaherty processed his film on site so that he could show his Inuit collaborators and friends the images that were being made. From 1940, when he got his first camera, until his death in 1973, Pitseolak took hundreds of photographs (as well as making drawings and paintings). The images, many of which he processed in an igloo built for the purpose, document life in an Inuit camp, with portraits of his family, people who visited, the dogs, some animals and the many pictures of agents and agencies of change – the ship that came from the south to pick up those infected with TB, the first planes that arrived, a helicopter. Accounts of this work often insist that Pitseolak is motivated by a sense that his

world, the 'traditional' Inuit society he was born into, is disappearing. So he wishes to put it on record, to defy its disappearance with images. Mementos for everyone of what is to be lost. I wonder if this so: the photographs seem to be those of a photographer who delighted in making pictures, who enjoyed the making of what is a kind of huge family album.

Pitseolak is not the only person of the North to take these kinds of photographs. When visiting old and partially abandoned camp sites in the High Arctic in the 1970s and going into houses that families had left in order to be with their children who had been forced to go to school in the new settlements, I often noticed family snapshots pinned to the walls or lying in a small heap on a shelf or in a cardboard box. Cheap and basic cameras had come into the North not long before and had soon been used for the pleasure of making pictures of people. Family snapshots. The very opposite of the images of explorers and exploration.

This contrast, between the kinds of photographs that Inuit liked to take and the representations of exploration, is understandable enough. There is no mystery, nor any right and wrong, in the choices that are made by those who create these images or become images. There is, though, the huge difference between frontier and homeland, between journeys into the wild and journeys with people who live in this place. Of course there is pretence and posturing in photography; there are all kinds of misrepresentation at work in this particular way of representing. These are part of the fascination of such images, part of the delight we can take in both those who make journeys and the journeys they make. In the polar regions there is always the light, the beauty, the huge horizons, the extremity of geography. These are poles, extremes and outer edges by definition. The Antarctic and Arctic are indeed places for heroes and heroism. Just as the North is a set of places where hunters and gatherers have created their anti-heroism, their cultures and domesticity. The delight of any collection of work that goes in both these directions is the delight in it all.

London, 2008

RIGHT: Shackleton on deck, one of the last photographs taken of him, *Quest* expedition, 1921.

ABOVE: Unpublished photographs of Wally Herbert and Allan Gill's attempted circumnavigation of Greenland, July 1979.

RIGHT: *Terra Nova's* crew take advantage of a sheltered spot to nap and read in the sunshine, December 1910.

FURTHER READING

Useful accounts of the art of the photograph are numerous. This list is intended as an overview of a broad subject. From the moment that photographs are taken they go on many journeys and this is reflected in the ways that people write about them. The application of photography to exploration deserves further study.

• Gerry Badger, *The Genius of Photography: How Photography Has Changed Our Lives* (London: Quadrille, 2007).

• Cecil Beaton and Gail Buckland, *The Magic Image: The Genius of Photography from 1839 to the Present Day* (London: Weidenfeld and Nicolson, 1975).

• Michael Bell, 'Thomas Mitchell, Photographer and Artist in the High Arctic, 1875-76', *Image*, 15 (1972), 12-21.

• William Bradford, *The Arctic Regions, Illustrated with Photographs Taken on an Art Expedition to Greenland, with Descriptive Narrative by the Artist* (London: S. Low, Marston, Low, and Searle, 1873).

• Graham Clarke, ed., *The Portrait in Photography* (London: Reaktion, 1992).

• Richard G. Condon, 'The History and Development of Arctic Photography', *Arctic Anthropology*, 26 (1989), 46-87.

• Jonathan Crary, *Techniques of the Observer: Vision and Modernity in the Nineteenth Century* (Ithaca: Cornell University Press, 1991).

• Rainer Fabian and Hans-Christian Adam, *Masters of Early Travel Photography, 1839-1919* (London: Thames and Hudson, 1983).

• Peter Geller, *Northern Exposures: Photographing and Filming the Canadian North, 1920-45* (Vancouver: University of British Columbia Press, 2004).

• Helmut Gernsheim, *The History of Photography: From the Camera Obscura to the Beginning of the Modern Era* (London: Thames and Hudson, 1969).

• Helmut Gernsheim, *The Rise of Photography, 1850-1880: The Age of Collodion* (London: Thames and Hudson, 1988).

• Vicki Goldberg, *The Power of Photography: How Photographs Changed Our Lives* (London: Abbeville Press, 1991).

• Adam Greenhalgh, 'The Not So Truthful Lens: William Bradford's *The Arctic Regions*', in *William Bradford: Sailing Ships and Arctic Seas*, edited by Richard C. Kugler (Seattle: University of Washington Press, 2003).

• Jennifer Green-Lewis, *Framing the Victorians: Photography and the Culture of Realism* (Ithaca: Cornell University Press, 1996).

• James Hannavy, *Victorian Photographers at Work* (Buckinghamshire: Shire Publications, 1997).

• Mark Haworth-Booth, ed., *The Golden Age of British Photography, 1839-1900* (New York: Aperture, 1984).

• Heinz Henisch and Bridget Henisch, *The Photographic Experience 1839-1914: Images and Attitudes* (University Park: Pennsylvania State University Press, 1994).

• Robert Hershkowitz, *The British Photographer Abroad: The First Thirty Years* (London: Hershkowitz, 1980).

• Tom Hopkinson, *Treasures of the Royal Photographic Society, 1839-1919* (London: Heinemann, 1980).

• Anne-Celine Jaeger, *Image Makers, Image Takers: The Essential Guide to Photography By Those in The Know* (London: Thames and Hudson, 2007).

• Ian Jeffrey, *Photography: A Concise History* (London: Thames and Hudson, 1981).

• Max Jones, *The Last Great Quest: Captain Scott's Antarctic Sacrifice* (Oxford: Oxford University Press, 2003).

• Estelle Jussim, *Visual Communication and the Graphic Arts: Photographic Technologies in the Nineteenth Century* (New York: Xerox Publications, 1974).

• J.C.H. King and Henrietta Lidchi, eds., *Imaging the Arctic* (London: British Museum, 1998).

• Suren Lalvani, *Photography, Vision, and the Production of Modern Bodies* (Albany: State University of New York Press, 1996).

• Jean-Claude Lemagny and André Rouillé, eds., *A History of Photography: Social and Cultural Perspectives* (Cambridge: Cambridge University Press, 1987).

• George Lowe, 'Thirty-Below-Zero: Photography at the Bottom of the World', *Kodak View*, 2 (1958), 1-6.

• Gus Macdonald, *Camera: A Victorian Eye Witness* (London: B.T. Batsford, 1979).

• Willem Mörzer Bruyns, 'Photography in the Arctic, 1876-84: The Work of W.J.A. Grant', *Polar Record*, 39:209 (2003), 123-30.

• Beaumont Newhall, *The History of Photography from 1839 to the Present Day* (New York: Museum of Modern Art, 1949).

• Herbert Ponting, 'Cinematographing in the Antarctic', *Pearson's Magazine*, 38:225 (1914), 235-49.

• Herbert Ponting, *The Great White South: Being an Account of Experiences with Captain's Scott's South Pole Expedition and of the Nature Life in the Antarctic* (London: Duckworth, 1921).

• Jan Piggott, ed., Shackleton: *The Antarctic and Endurance* (London: Dulwich College, 2000).

• Beau Riffenburgh and Liz Cruwys, *The Photographs of H.G. Ponting* (London: The Discovery Gallery, 1998).

• Royal Geographical Society, *To the Ends of the Earth, Visions of a Changing World: 175 Years of Exploration and Photography* (London: Bloomsbury, 2005).

• James R. Ryan, 'Images and Impressions: Printing, Reproduction and Photography', in *The Victorian Vision: Inventing New Britain*, edited by John M. Mackenzie (London: V&A Publications, 2001).

• James R. Ryan, *Picturing Empire: Photography and the Visualization of the British Empire* (London: Reaktion, 1997).

• Ann Savours, ed., *Scott's Last Voyage: Through the Antarctic Camera of Herbert Ponting* (London: Sidgwick and Jackson, 1974).

• Joan M. Schwartz and James R. Ryan, eds., *Picturing Place: Photography and Imaginative Geographies* (London: I.B. Tauris, 2003).

• Grace Seiberling, *Amateurs, Photography and the Mid-Victorian Imagination* (Chicago: University of Chicago Press, 1986).

• W.A. Somerset, 'A Slave of the Ruby Lamp: How Frank Hurley Became a World-Famous Photographer', *Life Magazine*, (1919), 161-67.

• Susan Sontag, *On Photography* (London: Allen Lane, 1978).

• *South with Endurance: Shackleton's Antarctic Expedition 1914-1917* (London: Bloomsbury, 2001).

• John Taylor, *A Dream of England: Landscape, Photography and the Tourist's Imagination* (Manchester: Manchester University Press, 1994).

• *The Shackleton Voyages: A Pictorial Anthology of the Polar Explorer and Edwardian Hero* (London: Weidenfeld and Nicolson, 2002).

• Alan Thomas, *The Expanding Eye: Photography and the Nineteenth-Century Mind* (London: Croom Helm, 1977).

• Douglas Wamsley and William Barr, 'Early Photographers of the Arctic', *Polar Record*, 32:183 (1996), 295-316.

• Mike Weaver, ed., *The Art of Photography, 1839-1989* (New Haven: Yale University Press, 1989).

• Mike Weaver, ed., *British Photography in the Nineteenth Century: The Fine Art Tradition* (Cambridge: Cambridge University Press, 1989).

• *With Scott to the Pole: The Terra Nova Expedition, 1910-1913* (London: Bloomsbury, 2004).

INDEX

PICTURE CREDITS

Scott Polar Research Institute: front cover, 2, 5, 6-7, 10-11, 14, 17, 18-19, 20, 26, 31, 32-33, 34-35, 36, 37, 38, 40, 43, 44-45, 46, 48, 49, 52, 57, 60-61, 64, 69, 73, 77, 80, 84, 88, 92, 96, 101, 109, 112, 120, 128, 132, 136-37, 145, 148, 149, 152, 153, 156, 157, 160-61, 164-65, 172, 176, 181, 185, 188-89, 193, 196, 197, 198, 205, 208-09, 213, 221, 225, 229, 232, 232-33, 236, 240, 244, 245, 252, 254, 255, 256-57, 257, 258, 259, 261, 272-73, 276, 278, 281, 283, 284-85, 286-87, 288, back cover.
Martin Hartley: 6-7, 8-9, 12-13, 46, 50-51, 54-55, 58-59, 62-63, 66-67, 70-71, 74-75, 78-79, 83, 86-87, 90, 91, 95, 98-99, 102, 103, 110-11, 114-15, 118-19, 123, 127, 131, 134-35, 139, 142, 147, 150-51, 154-55, 158-59, 163, 166, 167, 170-71, 175, 178-79, 182, 186, 190, 191, 194, 202, 203, 206-07, 210-11, 214-15, 218-19, 222, 226-27, 230, 235, 238-39, 247, 248-49, 250, 258, 259, 260, 262, 263, 265, 266, 268, 269, 270, 271, 274, 277, 286-87, back cover.
Huw Lewis-Jones: 23, 24, 25, 26, 27, 29, 36, 39, 41, 42, 116, 217.
Sir Wally Herbert: 124, 141, 168, 201, 282.
Arctic Kingdom: 242-43.
Hugh Brody: 279.
HSH Albert II, Sovereign Prince of Monaco: 104, 105, 106-07.

Wherever possible, when there is any doubt, effort has been made to identify the current copyright holders of imagery.

ACKNOWLEDGEMENTS

We would like to thank Arctic Kingdom for their support of this project.

Huw Lewis-Jones: Thanks to everyone who made this possible, in particular the library and museum team at SPRI, my friends and family, to my mother for her unquestioning support, to lovely Kari Herbert, and to my late grandfather who opened my eyes to the polar regions.

Martin Hartley: Thanks to my Dad, for buying my first camera, my mother for being so outwardly proud, to Natasha for her patience, and to Mark How of the How Trust for my first polar expedition in 2002.

LEFT: Robert Scott, George Simpson, Henry Bowers and Teddy Evans leaving on 'a remarkably pleasant and instructive little spring journey' to the Western Mountains, 15 September 1911. It was probably on this trip that Scott picked his companions for the push to the Pole.

BACK PAGE: Krisravista and the gramophone, *Terra Nova* expedition, 1910-13.